. . . . *Leader Guide* . . . .

"Wisdom That Transforms. Action That Lasts."

The Get Wisdom Commitment

At Get Wisdom Publishing we believe that true wisdom has the power to transform lives. Our mission is to equip readers with timeless insights and practical tools that inspire growth, guide decisions, and empower purposeful living. We don't just inform—we empower.

Our books combine profound understanding with real-life application, enabling readers to unlock their potential and navigate life's challenges with clarity and confidence. With each step guided by wisdom, we help you create lasting change and live the life you deserve.

When wisdom meets purpose, transformation follows.

. . . . *Leader Guide* . . . .

The *OBSCURE*
Bible Study Series

Grow in your faith through investigating unusual and obscure biblical characters.

"Deep Biblical Wisdom.
Real-Life Faith Application."

The OBSCURE Bible Study Journey

Meet Shamgar, Jethro, Manoah & Hathach	4 Lessons
Blasphemy, Grace, Quarrels & Reconciliation	8 Lessons
The Beginning and the End	8 Lessons
God at the Center	8 Lessons
Women of Courage	8 Lessons
The Beginning of Wisdom	8 Lessons
Miracles and Rebellion	8 Lessons
The Chosen People	8 Lessons
The Chosen Person	8 Lessons

. . . . *Leader Guide* . . . .

The Beginning and the End

From Creation to Eternity

Leader Guide
Book 3

Faith without application is incomplete.

Stephen H Berkey

GETWISDOM
PUBLISHING

COPYRIGHT

ISBN 978-1-7344094-8-2   (Leader Guide, paperback)

ISBN 978-1-9523590-0-2   (Leader Guide, ebook)

ISBN 978-1-7344094-9-9   (Personal Study Guide, paperback)

ISBN 978-1-9523590-1-9   (Personal Study Guide, ebook)

Audiobook available   (amazon.com and audible.com)

Bible Translations Used:

Discover the biblical characters that mainstream studies forget – and the timeless lessons they teach."

TABLE OF CONTENTS

CONTENTS

FREE PDF RESOURCES

Living Wisely
The Life Planning Guide

A Quick-Start Guide to Purposeful Living and Wise Decisions!

Discover the five life domains: purpose, people, principles, productivity, and perspective. Wisdom is the ability to apply truth and logic to real-life decisions and produce good outcomes. It influences your choices and will produce action that lasts. Consider and apply the five practical wisdom principles for daily living. (6 pages)

Free PDF: https://getwisdompublishing.com/resource-registration/

Living Wisely
The Life Planning Guide

Wisdom That Transforms.
Action That Lasts.

Stephen H Berkey
J.S. Wellman

Free PDF

Five Practical Principles For Life

When wisdom meets purpose, transformation follows.

Free PDF
Wise Decision-Making

[Get the ebook version for 99 cents]

You can make good choices.

This free resource provides a project-oriented perspective and gives ten detailed steps to analyze issues/problems to determine a solution. (26 pages)

Good decisions expand your horizons. Don't allow the fear of decision-making paralyze your ability to make good choices. Think through the reasonable alternatives and move forward. When your eyes are on the goal, making good decisions is easier.

Free PDF: https://getwisdompublishing.com/resource-registration/

Kindle ebook for 99 cents: https://www.amazon.com/dp/B09SYGWRVL/

Ebook

Free PDF

Make Thoughtful Decisions!

Good decisions expand your horizons.

Why Study OBSCURE Characters?

Unique, New, and Fresh

For experienced Bible students these characters will provide a fresh and interesting approach to Bible study. Since most of the material will be unfamiliar to the participants, new believers or those just starting Bible study should not feel intimidated by students who have been studying for years. Most readers will not be acquainted with the majority of the characters and events in this series.

Knowledge of Scripture

These studies are a great introduction for those just beginning Bible study. Regardless of their level of knowledge, everyone should find the characters and stories provide an opportunity to grow in their faith through investigating fascinating and unusual biblical stories and incidents.

Valuable Life Lessons

These lesser-known characters are a lot like you and me. God uses all sorts of people to accomplish His plans! You will become familiar with ordinary people, strange characters, and people living on the fringe of life who have the same troubles and challenges as people today. The deep truths and life lessons embedded in these studies should be valuable. They will provide new insights to scripture.

"Unlock Biblical Wisdom.
Transform Your faith!"

ABOUT THE LEADER GUIDE

General

This Guide is designed to give the Leader adequate information to effectively lead a discussion of each lesson. It contains additional information and background and follow-up questions.

You do <u>not</u> need to be a Bible student or mature Christian, to lead a group discussion with this Guide.

All you need is a desire and basic group facilitating skills. You simply need to read the questions aloud and keep the group discussion on target.

We recommend that you begin the discussion by reading the provided Scripture. This will allow time for everyone to get settled. It will remind everyone of the subject and bring their minds to a common focus. We do not believe ice-breakers are necessary given the unique nature of the material. If you sense that the group needs additional focus before you begin, conduct a <u>short</u> discussion about the themes of the lesson or ask about the meaning of a particular term.

Goals

The discussion should center around the themes and application questions at the end of the lesson. Your goal as the Leader should be to foster understanding and familiarity with Scripture. For new believers or participants who are not comfortable with the Bible, your goal should be to help them begin to seek knowledge and understanding from His Word. Try to get participants to put themselves into the lives of the *OBSCURE* character and feel what that character is feeling, thinking, or believing. More mature participants have the opportunity to dig deeper and find personal meaning and understanding. They may be particularly impacted by the Application questions.

Prayer

Unless you have an outstanding person of prayer in your group, you as the leader should wrap up your discussion time with prayer that specifically reflects the discussion and the themes, purpose, and focus of the lesson.

"Discover the Overlooked.
Apply it to Your Life!"

Book Description

Revitalize Your Faith: Fresh Perspectives on Timeless Biblical Truths

Do you believe in God, yet life feels overwhelmingly stressful? Do you sometimes wonder if God truly hears you amidst the chaos?

This book offers fresh perspectives on timeless biblical truths, revitalizing your faith and bringing peace to your soul. This transformative study from Get Wisdom Publishing helps you connect with God's bigger picture, replacing worry and stress with unwavering confidence in His plan for your life.

Learn to rely on God's wisdom rather than your own understanding. Find peace and contentment by surrendering your worries to Him. Cultivate a consistent daily Bible reading habit that enriches your spiritual life, drawing you closer to the heart of God. You'll walk alongside Eve, Lot's Wife, and other known and misunderstood characters to find confidence in your daily walk.

Why wait any longer to discover the power of applied wisdom? Bring fresh perspective to your studies with insights others have missed. This book will empower you to discover wisdom of Scripture and apply it to your everyday struggles.

This book presents four lessons from the Book of Genesis (the beginning) and four lessons from the Book of Revelation (the end). The book begins with Eve, who is certainly not an obscure character, but no one in the Garden of Eden is truly obscure. The book then examines Lot's wife, who turned into a pillar of salt, and Potiphar's wife, who tried to seduce Joseph. Because the beginning would not be complete if we ignored The Flood, we investigate the circumstances of Noah's family being saved although they were not deemed righteous.

The last four lessons are taken from the Book of Revelation: the Two Witnesses, The Woman who rides the Beast, the 24 Elders, and the New Jerusalem. These three interesting characters plus an event tell us a great deal about end times. The material is easy to understand and the student should leave the study with a much clearer understanding of end times events.

"Scripture holds answers in unexpected places. Our unique Bible studies reveal overlooked wisdom for today's challenges."

INTRODUCTION

*We equip readers with timeless wisdom and practical tools
that transform, not just inform. Our books combine
deep insights with real-life application
to create lasting change.*

Description of The OBSCURE Bible Study Series

This unique series uses a number of lesser-known Bible characters and events to explore such major themes as Angels, being Born Again, Courage, Death, Evangelism, Faithfulness, Forgiveness, Grace, Hell, Leadership, Miracles, the Remnant, the Sabbath, Salvation, Rebellion, Sovereignty, Thankfulness, Women, the World, Creation, and End Times.

The series as a whole provides both a broad and fresh understanding of the nature of God as we see Him act in the lives of people we've never examined before.

Most of the people chosen for these studies are unfamiliar because they are mentioned only a few times in Scripture – fifteen only once or twice. Others, although more familiar, are included because of their particular contribution to kingdom work.

For example, Scripture mentions Shamgar only twice. One verse in Judges 3:31 tells his story and 5:6 simply establishes a timeline and says nothing more about him. Then there is Nicodemus, with whom we associate the concept of being "born again." His name appears only 5 times, all in one short passage in the book of John. Eve, although obviously not obscure, is included in order to investigate the creation story.

Group Discussion or Individual Study

These studies can be done individually or in a small discussion group. The real value of the study is in the discussion questions. We all see life differently and the thoughts and ideas shared in a group will often lead to a richer understanding of the Scripture. The questions often require the participant to put himself (herself) in the mind or circumstances of that person in the Scriptures.

The commentary portion of the introductory material in each lesson is there to help clarify the passage and set the stage for the discussion questions. The questions are designed to help the student understand the meaning of the text itself and explore the kingdom implications from a personal point of view.

Ideal For Both New and Mature Bible Students

These lessons have three underlying questions:

- "Who is this person?"
- "What is happening here?"
- "What is the implication for my life?"

Because of the obscurity of the characters under study, chances are that even experienced participants with prior understanding of the lesson's theme will find fresh material to explore. Both new and long-time students will be challenged by the life lessons these unfamiliar characters can teach them.

Format of Lessons

Each lesson begins with the Scripture using the ESV translation followed by short sections titled "Context," "What Do We Know," and "Observations." The discussion questions are designed to help the student understand the subject and are followed by several application questions.

"We believe applied wisdom empowers life change. Our books provide clarity, inspiration, and tools to equip readers to live their best life."

Eve
the wife of Adam

Occurrences of "Eve" in the Bible: 2

Eve is mentioned only once by name in the Creation
story (Gen 1-3). She is mentioned in Gen 4:1 as the
mother of Cain and Abel. She is referred to another
18 times as "wife" or "woman." There are also two
references to Eve in the New Testament.

Themes: Creation; the Fall (original sin)

Scripture

<u>The Creation</u>
Genesis 1:1-2, 26-28, 31
*In the beginning, God created the heavens and the earth. 2 The
earth was without form and void, and darkness was over the face
of the deep. And the Spirit of God was hovering over the face of the
waters. . . . 26 Then God said, "Let us make man in our image, after
our likeness. And let them have dominion over the fish of the sea
and over the birds of the heavens and over the livestock and over all
the earth and over every creeping thing that creeps on the earth."
So God created man in his own image, in the image of God he
created him; male and female he created them. 28 And God
blessed them. And God said to them, "Be fruitful and multiply and
fill the earth and subdue it and have dominion over the fish of the
sea and over the birds of the heavens and over every living thing
that moves on the earth." . . . 31 And God saw everything that he
had made, and behold, it was very good. And there was evening
and there was morning, the sixth day. ESV*

Man in the Garden
Genesis 2:7, 15-17

then the Lord God formed the man of dust from the ground and breathed into his nostrils the breath of life, and the man became a living creature. . . .15 The Lord God took the man and put him in the garden of Eden to work it and keep it. 16 And the Lord God commanded the man, saying, "You may surely eat of every tree of the garden, 17 but of the tree of the knowledge of good and evil you shall not eat, for in the day that you eat of it you shall surely die." ESV

God Forms Woman
Genesis 2:22-25

And the rib that the Lord God had taken from the man he made into a woman and brought her to the man. 23 Then the man said, "This at last is bone of my bones and flesh of my flesh; she shall be called Woman, because she was taken out of Man." 24 Therefore a man shall leave his father and his mother and hold fast to his wife, and they shall become one flesh. 25 And the man and his wife were both naked and were not ashamed. ESV

Sin and Rebellion
Genesis 3:6-7

So when the woman saw that the tree was good for food, and that it was a delight to the eyes, and that the tree was to be desired to make one wise, she took of its fruit and ate, and she also gave some to her husband who was with her, and he ate. 7 Then the eyes of both were opened, and they knew that they were naked. And they sewed fig leaves together and made themselves loincloths. ESV

Consequences
Genesis 3:13, 16-17, 20-21

Then the Lord God said to the woman, "What is this that you have done?" The woman said, "The serpent deceived me, and I ate." . . . 16 To the woman he said, "I will surely multiply your pain in childbearing; in pain you shall bring forth children. Your desire shall be for your husband, and he shall rule over you." 17 And to Adam he said, "Because you have listened to the voice of your wife and have eaten of the tree of which I commanded you, 'You shall not eat of it,' cursed is the ground because of you; in pain you shall eat of it all the days of your life" . . . *20 The man called his wife's name Eve, because she was the mother of all living. 21 And the Lord God made for Adam and for his wife garments of skins and clothed them.* ESV

The Context

This was the Beginning! The word "genesis" means *origin, source,* or *the beginnings,* and the beginning starts with the Creation. The importance of beginnings can be illustrated by the following outline of the Bible that consists of only three subjects:

> Genesis 1-2   The Creation.
> Genesis 3   The Fall (Adam and Eve's original sin).
> Genesis 4   God reconciling man to Himself.

It is believed that Moses wrote the first five books of the Bible, including the book of Genesis, which would have been passed down orally through the generations to Moses.

What Do We Know About Creation?

There are two fundamental understandings we must take away from the Creation story in Gen 1-2:

> (1) <u>God exists</u>. God is the main character in this story. He existed "in the beginning" before He created the universe. The author of Hebrews describes it as follows:
>
> Heb 1:10-12   *"You, Lord, laid the foundation of the earth in the beginning, and the heavens are the work of your hands; 11 they will perish, but you remain; they will all wear out like a garment, 12 like a robe you will roll them up, like a garment they will be changed. But you are the same, and your years will have no end."* ESV
>
> (2) <u>God created all things</u>. He created the heavens, the earth, the water, the light, the plants, the creatures. He

created and formed everything. The Psalms confirm that God created the heavens and the earth out of nothing:

> Psalms 33:6, 9   *By the word of the Lord the heavens were made, and by the breath of his mouth all their host. . . . 9 For he spoke, and it came to be; he commanded, and it stood firm.* ESV

I am not really sure why some Christians want to argue about whether the days are 24 hour days or "ages." In my view that is not what most 21st century Christians need to take away from the Creation story. God created the universe and all that is in it, and it was "good." Then He created man in His own image and declared it was "very good" (1:31). Regardless of how this all happened or how long it took, the critical point for most disciples to understand and accept is that God did it.

Observations and Life Lessons

Why did God decide to provide Adam a helper? Gen 2:18 says that God determined it was not good for man to be alone. After He had made all the other living creatures (2:19-20), God declared that none of the creatures was the right or perfect complement for Adam. So God made man's helper from Adam's rib and Adam said:

> *"This at last is bone of my bones and flesh of my flesh; she shall be called Woman, because she was taken out of Man."*

What does the Bible mean when it describes the woman as a "helper"? Some try to make this statement imply she is a servant of man. I don't believe this statement refers to Eve's worth, value, or relative importance, but rather it describes the role she is to fulfill in her relationship to Adam. Remember, it is Adam who has the "problem:" he needs companionship because being alone is not good.

The Hebrew word used here for *helper* means to *surround, protect,* or *provide aid*. The meaning, therefore, strongly suggests the woman will provide relief and aid when Adam is in need. The

4

Holman translation includes the explanatory words that God provided woman as a "complement" to man, indicating that the addition of woman to the Creation scene made the whole better and man complete.

Inherently man needs relationships. Man was not made to be a loner: God Himself said it was not good to be alone. Because man was made in God's image, it follows that God desires relationship as well. And that may be one reason for the Trinity. If man needs "relationship" to the degree that the creatures and woman were formed to provide relationships for the first man, then that tells us a great deal about how God views relationship! We are made in His image and we have the same desire for relationship. Given this understanding, it is not surprising that God desires a relationship with us.

Discussion Questions

A. THE CREATION

A1. What do you think "In the beginning" means? When was that?

> *Before God created the heavens and the earth.
> *Not at the beginning of time (see 2:4).
> *Before anything that we know or understand as the universe.

A2. Genesis 1:26 says that God created man and woman "*in Our image, according to Our likeness.*" What do you think "image" and "likeness" mean? What are the implications? Do we look like God?

> *No, this is not about looks.
> *Humans are the only created beings made in God's image, but the text here does not refer to our physical appearance.
> *"Nature" might be a better word than "image" because the word "image" is so tied to a visual understanding. Man has many of the attributes of God; they are just not as

developed or perfected. Of, course we do not possess the exclusively divine attributes like omnipresence or omniscience.

*LEADER: This is an important question and it is critical that your group understand the inherent meaning. Our image or nature being like God would include such attributes as:

> *Inherent spiritual, emotional, intellectual nature.
> *Morals or values.
> *Ability to distinguish right from wrong.
> *Thinking and intellect.
> *Emotions.
> *Decision-making.
> *Ability to rule over the earth (see 1:28).
> *Our spiritual nature.
> *Our will.

B. GOD CREATED MAN

B1. What did God use to create Adam (2:7)?

> *Dust from the ground.
> *The earth (dirt) that He had previously created from nothing.
> *So man was created from something in existence that God had already created.
> *He was not made from <u>nothing</u> as the heavens and the earth, etc.

B2. What did God do to put life into Adam that He did not do for any of the other creatures?

> *He breathed the breath of life into nostrils.
>
> *Q. What is the significance of this creative act by God?
>
> > *Humans are of higher or greater worth (significance) than creatures.

*Breathing life into man was a <u>significantly personal gesture.</u>

C. GOD CREATED WOMAN

C1. What did God use to create Eve (2:21)?

*Adam's rib.
*She was taken from man (2:23).

C2. Why do you think Eve was formed from Adam and not from the earth like Adam?

*Be the same as man, but not be identical.
*Perfect fit, perfect match, same nature.
*Fit like hand and glove.
*Same inherent nature, therefore be compatible.

C3A. If you are a man, what would you expect when God says He is giving you a helper?

*Somebody to help with caring for the Garden.

C3B. If you are a woman, put yourself in Eve's position. What does it mean to you when you are told to be a helper to Adam?

*Partner in working (caring for garden).
*Partner in producing children.
*Partner in life.

*Q. Would your perception change if He said "helpmate"?

*Helper and helpmate have different meanings.

D. SIN

D1. When Adam and Eve ate the fruit, what wisdom do you think they received?

> *Knowledge is not wisdom.
> *They are <u>not</u> getting understanding or wisdom – they receive knowledge, which is intellectual information.
> *Such knowledge would produce awareness, curiosity, experimentation, etc.
> *They now know the difference between good and evil, how it impacts others, how it can be used selfishly, knowledge of sin (evil), etc.

D2. What is the difference between knowledge and wisdom?

> *Knowledge is knowing the facts or about the facts.
> *Wisdom is the application of knowledge or understanding to a specific end,
> *Wisdom allows understanding and ability to exercise good judgment in making right decisions in order to achieve the <u>correct</u> outcome.

D3. Is what Eve said in 3:3 accurate?
"But about the fruit of the tree in the middle of the garden, God said, 'You must not eat it or touch it, or you will die.'"

> *No . . . she added to what God told Adam.
> *God said nothing about touching.
> *Eve adds that she is not to touch it – maybe this is evidence that the serpent's distortions are having impact.
> *NOTE: Satan has won half the battle when he can lead people to confuse, question, or change God's Word.

*Q. How do you think that Eve knows she is not to eat from the tree?

> *We must assume Adam told her.
> *There is no report that God told her directly, but He could have.

D4. Why does 3:6 say that Eve ate the fruit?

> *Saw that good for *food*.
> *It was delightful to *look* at.
> *It seemed desirable for obtaining *wisdom*.

D5. Based on what Eve said she believed, what would have been her state of mind when she touched the fruit and did not die?

> *If she really thought that God said not to touch, then when she touched and did not die, she would have been emboldened to proceed to eat, concluding that the serpent was right.

D6. Why do you think Adam ate the fruit, particularly given that God had spoken to him directly about not eating it?

> *Eve did not physically die.
> *He could tell it was good to eat – it looked delicious (Adam was there).
> *It is difficult to know, maybe:
>
> > *He was foolish.
> > *He wanted to please Eve.
> > *She might have been very convincing!

D7. Why didn't Eve talk to God about the serpent's claims before eating?

> *She let her desires/emotions control her actions, rather than her mind/heart.
> *She stopped thinking and Adam did not stop her from acting on her desires.
> *Not <u>thinking</u> is a major failing of man. God gave us a brain and we fail to use it.

E. CONSEQUENCES

E1. What did Satan do in 3:5 to deceive Eve?
"In fact, God knows that when you eat it your eyes will be opened and you will be like God, knowing good and evil." (3:5)

> *He was suggesting a motive for why God would lie.
> *He was suggesting that God wanted to keep something good from them.

E2. If you were Eve and believed the serpent's lie to Eve at this point, how would that reflect on God? What would you now believe about God if you believed the serpent?

> *God is insecure and does not want us to have too much knowledge.
> *God is not trustworthy.
> *God has tried to deceive us.
> *God is hiding information from us.
> *God is withholding something good.

E3. When questioned by God, Eve said she was deceived by the serpent. Do you believe her? Why? Why not?

> *Yes, to some extent, but she doesn't even seem to consider God's warning or think about it.

*Blaming the serpent removes the responsibility from Eve and places it on Satan.
*This is a big problem today: We don't take responsibility for our actions and we blame others.

E4. Whose sin is worse: Eve who is deceived or Adam who chose to participate?

>   *It doesn't matter; they both chose to sin.
>   *God does not distinguish between the seriousness of sin – it is sin!
>   *Caution: This is another unimportant argument like the length of a creation day.

E5. What do you think 3:16 means that "your desire will be for your husband, yet he will rule over you"?

>   *Her sexual attraction for the man, and his leadership of her, will create difficult challenges in their lives.
>   *She will desire her husband, even when sin is destroying the marital relationship.
>   *The result can create anguish, torment, frustration, and even abuse as man tries to exert domination over his wife.

E6. Adam and Eve covered themselves with leaves in order to fix the sin problem. What should they have done?

>   *REPENT – CONFESS – ASK for FORGIVENESS

>   *1 John 1:9   *If we confess our sins, He is faithful and righteous to forgive us our sins and to cleanse us from all unrighteousness.*

F. APPLICATION

F1. Because we are created in God's image, we must consider how well we reflect that image. Do others see Christ in you?

F2. What is your immediate reaction when you get caught in a sin?

>   *Deny the sin or lie about it!
>   *Blame someone else.
>   *Refuse responsibility.
>   *Openly blame God.
>   *Hide, avoid, try to keep it secret.
>   *Stop associating with Christian friends.
>   *Make excuses: (a) that's just the way I am; (b) nobody's
>   perfect; (c) that's the way God made me.
>   *Confess, repent, and ask for forgiveness.

F3. Do you need to breathe life into your relationship with God?

F4. Do you need to be a better helper or partner in your marriage?

Lot's Wife
a pillar of salt

Occurrences of "Lot's wife" in the Bible: 4

Themes: Curiosity; Hesitation; Rebellion

Scripture

Genesis 13:12-13
Abram settled in the land of Canaan, while Lot settled among the cities of the valley and moved his tent as far as Sodom. 13 Now the men of Sodom were wicked, great sinners against the Lord. ESV

Genesis 18:20-24, 32
Then the Lord said, "Because the outcry against Sodom and Gomorrah is great and their sin is very grave, 21 I will go down to see whether they have done altogether according to the outcry that has come to me. And if not, I will know." 22 So the men turned from there and went toward Sodom, but Abraham still stood before the Lord. 23 Then Abraham drew near and said, "Will you indeed sweep away the righteous with the wicked? 24 Suppose there are fifty righteous within the city. Will you then sweep away the place and not spare it for the fifty righteous who are in it?" . . . 32 Then he said, "Oh let not the Lord be angry, and I will speak again but this once. Suppose ten are found there." He answered, "For the sake of ten I will not destroy it." ESV

Genesis 19:12-17
Then the men said to Lot, "Have you anyone else here? Sons-in-law, sons, daughters, or anyone you have in the city, bring them out of

the place. 13 For we are about to destroy this place, because the outcry against its people has become great before the Lord, and the Lord has sent us to destroy it." 14 So Lot went out and said to his sons-in-law, who were to marry his daughters, "Up! Get out of this place, for the Lord is about to destroy the city." But he seemed to his sons-in-law to be jesting. 15 As morning dawned, the angels urged Lot, saying, "Up! Take your wife and your two daughters who are here, lest you be swept away in the punishment of the city." 16 But he lingered. So the men seized him and his wife and his two daughters by the hand, the Lord being merciful to him, and they brought him out and set him outside the city. 17 And as they brought them out, one said, "Escape for your life. Do not look back or stop anywhere in the valley. Escape to the hills, lest you be swept away." ESV

Gen 19:23-26, 29

The sun had risen on the earth when Lot came to Zoar. 24 Then the Lord rained on Sodom and Gomorrah sulfur and fire from the Lord out of heaven. 25 And he overthrew those cities, and all the valley, and all the inhabitants of the cities, and what grew on the ground. 26 But Lot's wife, behind him, looked back, and she became a pillar of salt. . . . 29 So it was that, when God destroyed the cities of the valley, God remembered Abraham and sent Lot out of the midst of the overthrow when he overthrew the cities in which Lot had lived. ESV

New TestamentT Reference: Luke 17:28-33

Likewise, just as it was in the days of Lot – they were eating and drinking, buying and selling, planting and building, 29 but on the day when Lot went out from Sodom, fire and sulfur rained from heaven and destroyed them all – 30 so will it be on the day when the Son of Man is revealed. 31 On that day, let the one who is on the housetop, with his goods in the house, not come down to take them away, and likewise let the one who is in the field not turn back. 32 Remember Lot's wife. ESV

The Context

We often forget that the angels that rained destruction down on Sodom and Gomorrah are the same angels who only a few days earlier had told Abraham and Sarah they would have a son within a year.

The outcry due to Sodom and Gomorrah's sin was so great it had reached the ears of God. The sin of Sodom and Gomorrah had so impacted the people that it remained in the consciousness of the prophets for generations:

> Isaiah 3:9
> *For the look on their faces bears witness against them; they proclaim their sin like Sodom; they do not hide it. Woe to them! For they have brought evil on themselves.* ESV

> Ezekiel 16:49-50
> *Behold, this was the guilt of your sister Sodom: she and her daughters had pride, excess of food, and prosperous ease, but did not aid the poor and needy. 50 They were haughty and did an abomination before me. So I removed them, when I saw it.* ESV

> Zephaniah 2:9
> *"Therefore, as I live," declares the Lord of hosts, the God of Israel, "Moab shall become like Sodom, and the Ammonites like Gomorrah, a land possessed by nettles and salt pits, and a waste forever. The remnant of my people shall plunder them, and the survivors of my nation shall possess them."* ESV

What Do We Know?

We know in Gen 18:32 Abraham stopped negotiating with the Lord about the number of righteous people it would take for Him to spare Sodom and Gomorrah. We do not know why Abraham stopped at ten but it might have had something to do with the number of relatives Abraham had in the affected area. We know of

Lot and his wife and possibly two sons, along with at least two married daughters and their spouses (19:14) as well as at least two unmarried daughters (19:8). That would be ten people. As it turned out the group that fled from the city was reduced to only four: Lot, his wife, and two unmarried daughters. Lot's wife did not survive the dash to safety.

The end result is described as follows:

> Genesis 19:28-29   *And he* [Abraham] *looked down toward Sodom and Gomorrah and toward all the land of the valley, and he looked and, behold, the smoke of the land went up like the smoke of a furnace. 29 So it was that, when God destroyed the cities of the valley, God remembered Abraham and sent Lot out of the midst of the overthrow when he overthrew the cities in which Lot had lived.* ESV

Observations

Why did God save these four? Abraham's nephew, Lot, did not seem to be the sharpest guy on the block: he chose to live near sinful cities, he didn't listen very well, and he responded slowly. Divine mercy could be the reason Lot and some of his family were saved. Lot's wife did not survive, but that was her own fault: God's mercy had been made available and she chose to ignore the angel's commands.

> Titus 3:5   He *saved us, not because of works done by us in righteousness, but according to his own mercy, by the washing of regeneration and renewal of the Holy Spirit.* ESV

We do not know the full extent of the sin in Sodom and Gomorrah. We know about the rampant sexual immorality described in Gen 19:4-9. One can assume that people who live and act like this have no concern for basic human rights and freedoms. Ezekiel 16:49-50 tells us that the people were prideful, haughty, did not help the poor and needy even though they had the means, and did other "detestable things." People who have become so depraved that they will rape visitors for the fun of it are certainly capable of almost any sin you can imagine. One can only think that this is what it might have been like at the time of the Flood.

A New Testament reference (Luke 17:32) gives us another look at this story. Luke makes the point in the verses prior to Luke 17:32 that when the end times are upon us we should not be stalling for time, failing to be alert, or turning back for material and unnecessary things. If we fail to listen to God's instruction and are lax in responding, we might find ourselves saying, "*I should have better understood the message and warning when Lot's wife was turned to a pillar of salt!*"

Discussion Questions

A. LOT

A1. What is your general feeling about Lot? Would you characterize him as humble, quick to obey and pious, or do you find him slow, self-absorbed, and ineffective?

>   *Slow.
>   *Certainly wonder about his "righteousness."

A2. Based on Gen 19:29, why was Lot saved?
Genesis 19:29   *So it was that, when God destroyed the cities of the valley, God remembered Abraham and sent Lot out of the midst of the overthrow when he overthrew the cities in which Lot had lived.* ESV

>   *God remembered Abraham, meaning He honored His covenant relationship (Gen 18:18-19).
>   *God remembered his negotiations with Abraham.
>   *Lot was a "righteous" man (2 Peter 2:7).
>   *God did this more as a favor to Abraham than because of Lot's righteousness.

A3. Second Peter 2:7 says, *"and if He rescued righteous Lot, distressed by the unrestrained behavior of the immoral."* We must assume Lot is righteous, therefore, how would you explain Lot's behavior in all these events?

> *He was just slow, concerned about family and others; tended to push the envelope; not really openly rebellious.
> *He had a true feeling of responsibility for the people and the city – he was likely a leader (19:1).
> *He was influenced by his wife and family who were not righteous.

B. GENERAL

B1. Given Genesis 13:13, where the men in Sodom were described as evil, why did Lot pitch his tents near Sodom (13:12)?

> *Maybe wanted to participate in the activities of Sodom.
> *Maybe it was just unwise curiosity!
> *Maybe pride.
> *I am better than them, I can resist any temptation.
> *I am strong – their sin can't impact or influence me.
> *Maybe he was influenced by wife or family.
> *Maybe he wanted to be near the *action*!
> *Maybe he wanted to change the conditions.

B2. Is there anything wrong with choosing to live near Sodom?

> *Yes, you become who you associate with!
> *Proximity heightens the possibility of falling into temptation.
> *It is an outward appearance of support for sinful life style.
> *Even the best of intentions can be derailed when you are living in and among evil!

B3. Why do you think Abraham was concerned about Sodom and Gomorrah?

> *He was concerned primarily about the righteous people.
> *He was actually concerned about Lot and his family.
> *Abraham had compassion for the people.
> *He was concerned for the beautiful land which would be destroyed.
> *All of the above.

B4. What reason did Abraham have to believe that innocent and righteous people were living in these cities?

> *Probably none!
> *He only knew that Lot and family were living near Sodom.
> *It's likely he was really concerned about Lot, and only worried about the others because of his compassionate character.

B5. Do you think Abraham was out of line pleading for Sodom and Gomorrah? Why? Why not?

> *We are told that *"The outcry against Sodom and Gomorrah is immense, and their sin is extremely serious."*
> *One might think Abraham is being presumptuous.
> *If there really were righteous people there, God would know it and take appropriate steps consistent with His character.
> *God doesn't need Abraham to inform Him!

B6. Why wouldn't Abraham want God to demonstrate His power to the sinful people? Wouldn't the powerful display and destruction of evil give Abraham something to boast about?

> *It would be easy to sit back and let God destroy this evil.
> *But Abraham is apparently very concerned.

B7. What can we assume by the fact that Abraham started his negotiation at 50 and went down to 10?

> *He probably knew how bad it was and suspected he could not find many. Therefore, God was likely to accept this higher number knowing that Abraham could not find this many, allowing Abraham to continue to ask God to lower the number.
> *Abraham probably knew he wanted to get to 10 because that was the number in Lot's family.
>
> Q. Why didn't Abraham start at 5 and work up?
>
> *I would have!
> *His approach seems backward to me.

B8. Gen 19:16 says that Lot hesitated. Why would he hesitate?
Genesis 19:15-16   *As morning dawned, the angels urged Lot, saying, "Up! Take your wife and your two daughters who are here, lest you be swept away in the punishment of the city." 16 But he lingered. So the men seized him and his wife and his two daughters by the hand, the Lord being merciful to him, and they brought him out and set him outside the city. ESV*

> *Reluctant to leave his possessions.
> *Even though he was righteous, there was still strong attraction to the world and its values.
> *Maybe he liked danger.
> *Maybe the influence of his wife and family.
> *Since he was at city gate (19:1), implying a leader, he may have felt responsible for people and city, and he may have felt he was abandoning his responsibility.

B9. The angels did not take Lot and his wife to complete safety. They most certainly had the ability to take them to the mountains (or Zoar), but they only took them outside the city. Why? Is there a life lesson here?

*God will not do everything, We need to help, be willing, and make good choices.
*If we want to go to hell, He will allow us to make that decision.

B10. Do you find it curious that Gen 19:1 implies that Lot was a leader, elder, or official in Sodom?

*Leaders were normally at the city gate giving instruction and judging disputes.
*Yes, Lot seems to have been integrated into the fabric of Sodom far more than a righteous man would be.

B11. Why do you think Lot could not convince his own family that destruction was about to happen?
Genesis 19:14   *So Lot went out and said to his sons-in-law, who were to marry his daughters, "Up! Get out of this place, for the Lord is about to destroy the city." But he seemed to his sons-in-law to be jesting.* ESV

*Lot was an unreliable witness for the Lord.
*Lot did a poor job in trying to convince them.
*They had no real relationship with Lot that would convince them to believe his warning.
*He was not respected.
*They were not righteous men and God hardened their hearts.
*They did not qualify for being saved; no godly discernment.
*They may have sided with Lot's wife on matters of spiritual discernment.

B12. Why do you think Lot's wife stopped and looked back? What is the significance of that? What was the wife's problem?

>   *Unbelief and sadness for Sodom.
>   *Rebellion, stubbornness and defiance.
>   *Maybe there was some degree of drawing toward the lifestyle (sin) that existed in Sodom.
>   *Curiosity.

C. DIGGING DEEPER

C1. Do you think that Abraham really wanted justice?
Genesis 18:25   *Far be it from you to do such a thing, to put the righteous to death with the wicked, so that the righteous fare as the wicked! Far be that from you! Shall not the Judge of all the earth do what is just?* ESV

>   *No. What Abraham really wanted was mercy, not justice.
>   *Justice would result in people getting what they deserve.

C2. Why do you think Abraham would say this to God (Gen 18:25)?

>   *He was confused about corporate justice and individual justice. For example, not everyone who was exiled to Assyria and Babylon was unrighteous.
>   *He was concerned about his family.

C3. Can you think of examples when God:

Saved the righteous?

>   *Exodus: Angel of Death passed over doors with blood.
>   *The Flood: Noah was saved.

Allowed them to perish?

> *The defeat at Ai.
> *People exiled to Assyria and Babylon.

C4. Luke 17:32 says to "Remember Lot's wife." What do you think that means? What should we remember?

> *She rebelled and did not listen to God.
> *She did what she wanted – result was death.
> *She ignored God – never produces a good result.
> *She was self-absorbed.

C5. If Scripture said, "Remember Lot" (instead of Lot's wife) what would you take it to mean?

> *Although God will destroy the ungodly, he will also rescue the righteous.

C6. If someone said that God demonstrated "extravagant mercy" in His willingness to spare these cities if only ten righteous people were found, how would you respond? Would this seem right or logical to you?

> *God is sovereign: He can be merciful, just, or generous. He can choose to do what He wants, when He wants, and if He wants.
> *My finite mind does not have enough wisdom to determine appropriate action.
> *It demonstrates how much love and compassion God has and how far He will go to accommodate His people.
>
> Q. Can you think of any other times God demonstrated "extravagant mercy"?

> *He saved me!

C7. In reviewing Gen 19:15-20 we see that:

> 1) Lot and his family had not heeded the warnings.
> 2) Lot continually hesitated when told to leave.
>
> 3) Angels had to physically take the hands of the family and physically move them outside the city.
> 4) Lot negotiated with them to flee only to Zoar.

What, if anything, can you conclude from Lot's actions above?

> *Lot did not listen very well.
> *Lot did not take instruction well.
> *His actions came close to open rebellion.
> *Lot wanted the easy way - his way.
> *Lot had no control over his family.

D. APPLICATION

D1. Are you <u>really</u> listening to what God is saying? Or are you listening for what you want to hear?

D2. What do you feel strongly enough about that you would attempt to negotiate with God?

D3. Do you ever feel like ignoring God? What happens?

Potiphar's Wife
and Pharaoh's cupbearer

Occurrences of "Potiphar's wife" in Genesis 39: 4
Occurrences of "cupbearer" in Genesis 40-41: 10

Themes: Divine appointments; Divine events

Scripture

Genesis 39:7-9, 19-20   Potiphar's Wife
And after a time his master's wife cast her eyes on Joseph and said, "Lie with me." 8 But he refused and said to his master's wife, "Behold, because of me my master has no concern about anything in the house, and he has put everything that he has in my charge. 9 He is not greater in this house than I am, nor has he kept back anything from me except yourself, because you are his wife. How then can I do this great wickedness and sin against God?" . . . 19 As soon as his master heard the words that his wife spoke to him, "This is the way your servant treated me," his anger was kindled. 20 And Joseph's master took him and put him into the prison, the place where the king's prisoners were confined, and he was there in prison. ESV

Genesis 40:1-5   Pharaoh's Cupbearer
Sometime after this, the cupbearer of the king of Egypt and his baker committed an offense against their lord the king of Egypt. 2 And Pharaoh was angry with his two officers, the chief cupbearer and the chief baker, 3 and he put them in custody in the house of the captain of the guard, in the prison where Joseph was confined. 4 The captain of the guard appointed Joseph to be with them, and he attended them. They continued for some time in custody.

5 And one night they both dreamed—the cupbearer and the baker of the king of Egypt, who were confined in the prison—each his own dream, and each dream with its own interpretation. ESV

Genesis 40:12-15, 20-22   Joseph Interpret's the Cupbearer's Dream
Then Joseph said to him, "This is its interpretation: the three branches are three days. 13 In three days Pharaoh will lift up your head and restore you to your office, and you shall place Pharaoh's cup in his hand as formerly, when you were his cupbearer. 14 Only remember me, when it is well with you, and please do me the kindness to mention me to Pharaoh, and so get me out of this house. 15 For I was indeed stolen out of the land of the Hebrews, and here also I have done nothing that they should put me into the pit." . . . 20 On the third day, which was Pharaoh's birthday, he made a feast for all his servants and lifted up the head of the chief cupbearer and the head of the chief baker among his servants. 21 He restored the chief cupbearer to his position, and he placed the cup in Pharaoh's hand. 22 But he hanged the chief baker, as Joseph had interpreted to them. ESV

Genesis 41   Pharaoh's Dream
After two whole years, Pharaoh dreamed that he was standing by the Nile, 2 and behold, there came up out of the Nile seven cows attractive and plump, and they fed in the reed grass. 3 And behold, seven other cows, ugly and thin, came up out of the Nile after them, and stood by the other cows on the bank of the Nile. 4 And the ugly, thin cows ate up the seven attractive, plump cows. And Pharaoh awoke. 5 And he fell asleep and dreamed a second time. And behold, seven ears of grain, plump and good, were growing on one stalk. 6 And behold, after them sprouted seven ears, thin and blighted by the east wind. 7 And the thin ears swallowed up the seven plump, full ears. And Pharaoh awoke, and behold, it was a dream. 8 So in the morning his spirit was troubled, and he sent and called for all the magicians of Egypt and all its wise men. Pharaoh told them his dreams, but there was none who could interpret them to Pharaoh.

9 Then the chief cupbearer said to Pharaoh, "I remember my offenses today. 10 When Pharaoh was angry with his servants and put me and the chief baker in custody in the house of the captain of the guard, 11 we dreamed on the same night, he and I, each having a dream with its own interpretation. 12 A young Hebrew was there with us, a servant of the captain of the guard. When we told him, he interpreted our dreams to us, giving an interpretation to each man according to his dream. 13 And as he interpreted to us, so it came about. I was restored to my office, and the baker was hanged."

14 Then Pharaoh sent and called Joseph, and they quickly brought him out of the pit. And when he had shaved himself and changed his clothes, he came in before Pharaoh. 15 And Pharaoh said to Joseph, "I have had a dream, and there is no one who can interpret it. I have heard it said of you that when you hear a dream you can interpret it." 16 Joseph answered Pharaoh, "It is not in me; God will give Pharaoh a favorable answer." 17 Then Pharaoh said to Joseph, "Behold, in my dream I was standing on the banks of the Nile. 18 Seven cows, plump and attractive, came up out of the Nile and fed in the reed grass. 19 Seven other cows came up after them, poor and very ugly and thin, such as I had never seen in all the land of Egypt. 20 And the thin, ugly cows ate up the first seven plump cows, 21 but when they had eaten them no one would have known that they had eaten them, for they were still as ugly as at the beginning. Then I awoke. 22 I also saw in my dream seven ears growing on one stalk, full and good. 23 Seven ears, withered, thin, and blighted by the east wind, sprouted after them, 24 and the thin ears swallowed up the seven good ears. And I told it to the magicians, but there was no one who could explain it to me."

25 Then Joseph said to Pharaoh, "The dreams of Pharaoh are one; God has revealed to Pharaoh what he is about to do. 26 The seven good cows are seven years, and the seven good ears are seven years; the dreams are one. 27 The seven lean and ugly cows that came up after them are seven years, and the seven empty ears blighted by the east wind are also seven years of famine. 28 It is as I told Pharaoh; God has shown to Pharaoh what he is about to do. 29 There will come seven years of great plenty throughout all the land of Egypt, 30 but after them there will arise seven years of famine, and all the plenty will be forgotten in the land of Egypt. The famine will consume the land, 31 and the plenty will be unknown in the land by reason of the famine that will follow, for it will be very

severe. 32 And the doubling of Pharaoh's dream means that the thing is fixed by God, and God will shortly bring it about. 33 Now therefore let Pharaoh select a discerning and wise man, and set him over the land of Egypt. 34 Let Pharaoh proceed to appoint overseers over the land and take one-fifth of the produce of the land of Egypt during the seven plentiful years. 35 And let them gather all the food of these good years that are coming and store up grain under the authority of Pharaoh for food in the cities, and let them keep it. 36 That food shall be a reserve for the land against the seven years of famine that are to occur in the land of Egypt, so that the land may not perish through the famine." ESV

Genesis 42:2, 8   Joseph's Brothers in Egypt
And he said, "Behold, I have heard that there is grain for sale in Egypt. Go down and buy grain for us there, that we may live and not die.". . . 8 And Joseph recognized his brothers, but they did not recognize him. ESV

Genesis 45:3-5   Joseph and Brothers Reunited
And Joseph said to his brothers, "I am Joseph! Is my father still alive?" But his brothers could not answer him, for they were dismayed at his presence. 4 So Joseph said to his brothers, "Come near to me, please." And they came near. And he said, "I am your brother, Joseph, whom you sold into Egypt. 5 And now do not be distressed or angry with yourselves because you sold me here, for God sent me before you to preserve life." ESV

Genesis 45:16-20   Jacob Moves to Egypt
When the report was heard in Pharaoh's house, "Joseph's brothers have come," it pleased Pharaoh and his servants. 17 And Pharaoh said to Joseph, "Say to your brothers, 'Do this: load your beasts and go back to the land of Canaan, 18 and take your father and your households, and come to me, and I will give you the best of the land of Egypt, and you shall eat the fat of the land.' 19 And you, Joseph, are commanded to say, 'Do this: take wagons from the land of Egypt for your little ones and for your wives, and bring your father, and come. 20 Have no concern for your goods, for the best of all the land of Egypt is yours.'" ESV

The Context

The patriarchs of the first three generations of the Israelite nation are frequently mentioned together and it is usually related to Yahweh being the God of Abraham, Isaac, and Jacob. The covenant that God made with Abraham was reconfirmed to both Isaac and Jacob, the latter being the father of the Twelve Tribes of Israel.

In this study the subject is Joseph and how his life experiences brought him to Egypt which ultimately resulted in the relocation of Jacob and his whole family to Egypt. God had a plan for Israel and part of that plan was to grow them into a large nation. God's first priority was to get Jacob's family to Egypt. He accomplished that task through generating a series of divine appointments and events, beginning with Joseph's brothers selling Joseph to Ishmaelite traders on their way to Egypt.

What Do We Know?

When the story began in Genesis 37, Jacob and his entire family were living in Canaan. When the story ends in Genesis 47, Jacob and the Israelites were settled in the land of Goshen in Egypt. Many good and bad things happened between the beginning and end of the story, but through it all God was accomplishing His plan to bring Jacob and his family to Egypt where they could grow in size and ultimately become a mighty nation. This sophisticated scheme was designed to take Jacob and his family from the Promised Land in Canaan to Egypt, where they would stay for some 400 years.

We will examine a number of different events that took place so that God's plans were fulfilled. These were not accidents or coincidences. At the time, the players in God's drama had no idea that they were players in His plan to bring Jacob and his family to Egypt and enslave them, allowing them to grow into a large nation that God could bring back to the Promised Land under Moses' leadership.

Observations

There could be several answers to the question, "What is the meaning in this story?" The meaning will be different if we are looking at the entire experience of Joseph or just one portion of his life. The enslavement of the nation allowed them to grow in size and to _remain together_. Tribes, families, or individuals were not allowed to leave Egypt and the people survived through the care and comfort of each other. They all lived under similar circumstances and had a common antagonist: Egypt. But most importantly from God's perspective, they remained together.

Thus, when the Exodus occurred they had a common bond and common desire to escape and they had to rely on God. God used the exodus to mold His Chosen People into a nation. When they reached Sinai they were prepared (excluding the golden calf and all the grumbling) to be formed into a nation whose King was Yahweh.

But all this depended on Jacob moving to Egypt and staying there. We will see in this study how God arranged all that to happen.

Discussion Questions

A. JOSEPH AND BROTHERS IN CANAAN

DIVINE EVENT:
Genesis 37:3   *Now Israel [Jacob] loved Joseph more than any other of his sons, because he was the son of his old age. And he made him a robe of many colors.* ESV

A1. How would this story have changed if Jacob had not loved Joseph more than his other sons and had not given Joseph a robe of many colors (Gen 37:3)?

> *Joseph's brothers would have had ordinary brotherly jealousy rather than deep hatred and resentment.

*They would not have tried to kill him and he would not have been sold to traders going to Egypt.

A2. How would this story have changed if Joseph had not told his brothers about the dreams indicating he would reign over them (Gen 37:6-11)?

*This probably produced the level of jealousy and hatred that led to violence.
*NOTE: Remember that the oldest son was the favored child in this society, so having a younger brother usurp the privilege of the elder son was outrageous.

A3. What if Jacob had not sent Joseph to Shechem (about 50 miles away) to check on his brothers who were pasturing their father's flocks?

*At that distance the brothers could harm Joseph with impunity.
*At that distance Jacob would have been unable to confirm the brother's reports about Joseph's death.

A4. What would have been the impact if Rueben had not spoken up in defense of Joseph (Gen 37:21)?

*Brothers probably would have killed Joseph rather than throw him in a pit.

A5. What would have been the impact if a caravan of Ishmaelites had not passed by on their way to Egypt?

*Joseph would have been left in the pit to die unless Rueben had come back to rescue him (Gen 37:22, 25).
*Joseph would not have been taken to Egypt, unless God arranged another method for him to get there.

DIVINE EVENT:

Genesis 37:36   *Meanwhile the Midianites had sold him in Egypt to Potiphar, an officer of Pharaoh, the captain of the guard.* ESV

A6. What would have been the impact if Joseph had not been sold to a person working for or related to the Pharaoh (Potiphar)?

> *Joseph would not have met Potiphar's wife who caused him to end up in prison.
> *NOTE: Ultimately, if Joseph had not gone to the King's prison he would not have been in a position to interpret Pharaoh's dreams.

B. POTIPHAR'S WIFE

DIVINE EVENT:

Genesis 39:2-3   *The Lord was with Joseph, and he became a successful man, and he was in the house of his Egyptian master. 3 His master saw that the Lord was with him and that the Lord caused all that he did to succeed in his hands.* ESV

B1. What would have happened if the Lord had not made Joseph successful so that he became Potiphar's personal assistant?

> *He would not have met Potiphar's wife.

DIVINE EVENT:

Genesis 39:7-8   *And after a time his master's wife cast her eyes on Joseph and said, "Lie with me." 8 But he refused . . .* ESV

*__LEADER:__ Following are questions you might ask if there is extra time for discussion

> *Q. What are possible scenarios of how Joseph and Potiphar's wife might have related to each other after this event?

>   *Potiphar's wife ignored Joseph.
>   *Wife realized that Joseph would not sin against his God by sleeping with her.
>   *Joseph slept with Potiphar's wife.
>   *Potiphar did not care if Joseph slept with wife.
>   *Joseph left the area.

*Q. What are the possible actions Potiphar might have taken if he had known his wife was lying about Joseph?

>   *Joseph relocated away from wife.
>   *Potiphar chastised the wife and confined her in some way.
>   * Potiphar sent wife to another residence.
>   * Potiphar imprisoned Joseph.
>   *Potiphar killed Joseph.

B2. What reason did Joseph give for not accepting Potiphar's wife's advances?

>   *Loss of Potiphar's trust.
>   *It would be disloyal.
>   *Sin against his God.

*Q. Why isn't this a sin against Potiphar?

>   *Technically it's both, but the definition of sin is transgression against God's laws.

C. JOSEPH in PRISON

DIVINE EVENT:

Genesis 39:20   *And Joseph's master took him and put him into the prison, the place where the king's prisoners were confined, and he was there in prison. ESV*

C1. What would have happened if Joseph had not been placed in this particular prison?

> *This was the prison where the King's (Pharaoh) prisoners were confined.
> *This is an important divine circumstance because it was where the king's baker and cupbearer would be taken when they fell out of favor with Pharaoh.

DIVINE EVENT:
Genesis 39:21   *But the Lord was with Joseph and showed him steadfast love and gave him favor in the sight of the keeper of the prison.* ESV

C2. What would have happened if Joseph had not been granted favor in the eyes of the warden because the Lord had made everything he did successful (Gen 39:21-23)?

> *He would not have had the opportunity to meet the other prisoners in the prison (particularly the cupbearer).

C3. What would have happened if the Pharaoh had not imprisoned his baker and cupbearer in the place where Joseph was also confined?

> *Joseph would not have met them.

C4. What would have happened if the baker and cupbearer had not had dreams?

> *Joseph would not have had the opportunity to interpret their dreams.
> *The cupbearer would not have known that Joseph's God could interpret dreams.

DIVINE EVENT:
Genesis 40:8   *They said to him, "We have had dreams, and there is no one to interpret them." And Joseph said to them, "Do not interpretations belong to God? Please tell them to me."* ESV

C5. What would have happened if God had not interpreted the dreams for Joseph?

> *The cupbearer would have had no reason to remember Joseph when the Pharaoh had difficult dreams.

DIVINE EVENT:
Genesis 40:23   *Yet the chief cupbearer did not remember Joseph, but forgot him.* ESV

C6. What is the important result of the cupbearer not immediately remembering Joseph to the Pharaoh as he had promised (Gen 40:14, 23)?

> *Joseph stayed in prison where he could easily be found by the Pharaoh two years later when needed.

C7. What would have happened if the cupbearer had not remembered Joseph when Pharaoh had his dream?

> *Joseph would not have been brought in to interpret Pharaoh's dream and it would have been interpreted incorrectly by someone else.

C8. Why do you think that Pharaoh was pleased and believed that the interpretation was correct? What would Pharaoh lose if Joseph were wrong?

> <u>Why pleased:</u>
> *Joseph's <u>God</u> interpreted the dream through Joseph.
> *Seemed reasonable.
> *What choice did Pharaoh have?

What if wrong:
*He couldn't really be wrong because it was God who both gave the dream and interpreted it.
*It could only go wrong in the execution of the plan by Joseph:

(a) He didn't accumulate enough excess.
(b) Famine was far worse than Joseph planned for.

C9. What if the interpretation was right but the famine was much worse than Joseph expected?

*Pharaoh would have taken his share, but the people would have suffered.
*Egypt would survive but have no excess to sell to outsiders and other nations – in which case Jacob would not have sent his sons to buy food.

D. JACOB AND FAMILY

DIVINE EVENT:
Genesis 42:6-7   *Now Joseph was governor over the land. He was the one who sold to all the people of the land. And Joseph's brothers came and bowed themselves before him with their faces to the ground. 7 Joseph saw his brothers and recognized them . . .* ESV

D1. What would have happened if Joseph had not seen or recognized his brothers in all the hundreds and maybe thousands of people that were coming to buy food?

*Jacob would not have learned Joseph was alive and would not have come to Egypt to see his son.
*It was a God thing!

DIVINE EVENT:

Pharaoh instructed Joseph to bring his family to Egypt.

D2. What would have happened if Pharaoh had not invited Joseph's family to move to Egypt (45:16-18)?

> *God's plans and purposes for getting Jacob and his family to Egypt would have been delayed or another scenario would have had to occur.

D3. Do you think what occurred in 46:1 is significant? Why?

Genesis 46:1 *So Israel* [Jacob] *took his journey with all that he had and came to Beersheba, and offered sacrifices to the God of his father Isaac.* ESV

> *Yes, maybe even critical!
> *Jacob worshiped God and then God spoke to him in a vision.
> *I doubt that this is all coincidence. Jacob's relationship with God meant he gave thanks and worshiped Him in the appropriate circumstances.
> *God was predisposed to help Jacob since Jacob knew God.

D4. Why do you think God executed this complicated scheme to get Jacob and his family to Egypt? Why didn't God just speak to Jacob like He spoke to Abraham, and tell him to go?

> *There would have been no story! The story is important, easy to remember, and displays God's intervening hand in the process.
> *Maybe God knew that Jacob would resist going to Egypt! He would not leave the Promised Land.

E. APPLICATION

E1. Do you believe in divine appointments today?
Why? Why not?

*__LEADER:__ Consider asking this question during the discussion.

E2. Have there been "divine appointments" in your life? If yes, list a few:

      a) _____.

      b) _____.

      c) _____.

      d) _____.

E3. Did you recognize these events as divine appointments at the time they occurred? Why? Why not?

E4. Do you pray for divine appointments? If you were going to pray for such appointments or events today, what would you pray?

      a) _____.

      b) _____.

      c) _____.

Shem, Ham & Japheth
Noah's sons

Occurrences of "Shem, Ham, Japheth"
in the Bible: 13/8/7
The sons are mentioned together 5 times, all in Genesis,
chapters 5-14. They are also referred to a number of times as "sons."

Theme: Grace

Scripture

The Flood: Noah Found Favor in the Eyes of the Lord
Genesis 6:5-13, 18   *The Lord saw that the wickedness of man was great in the earth, and that every intention of the thoughts of his heart was only evil continually. 6 And the Lord was sorry that he had made man on the earth, and it grieved him to his heart. 7 So the Lord said, "I will blot out man whom I have created from the face of the land, man and animals and creeping things and birds of the heavens, for I am sorry that I have made them." 8 But Noah found favor in the eyes of the Lord. ESV*

Noah and the Flood
9 These are the generations of Noah. Noah was a righteous man, blameless in his generation. Noah walked with God. 10 And Noah had three sons, Shem, Ham, and Japheth. 11 Now the earth was corrupt in God's sight, and the earth was filled with violence. 12 And God saw the earth, and behold, it was corrupt, for all flesh had corrupted their way on the earth. 13 And God said to Noah, "I have determined to make an end of all flesh, for the earth is filled with violence through them. Behold, I will destroy them with the earth. . . . 18 But I will establish my covenant with you, and you shall come into the ark, you, your sons, your wife, and your sons' wives with you." ESV

Entering the Ark

Genesis 7:1, 13, 23   *Then the Lord said to Noah, "Go into the ark, you and all your household, for I have seen that you are righteous before me in this generation" . . . 13 On the very same day Noah and his sons, Shem and Ham and Japheth, and Noah's wife and the three wives of his sons with them entered the ark . . . 23 He blotted out every living thing that was on the face of the ground, man and animals and creeping things and birds of the heavens. They were blotted out from the earth. Only Noah was left, and those who were with him in the ark.* ESV

The Lord's Promise

Genesis 8:15-17   *Then God said to Noah, 16 "Go out from the ark, you and your wife, and your sons and your sons' wives with you. 17 Bring out with you every living thing that is with you of all flesh—birds and animals and every creeping thing that creeps on the earth—that they may swarm on the earth, and be fruitful and multiply on the earth."* ESV

Prophecies about Noah's Family

Genesis 9:18-19   *The sons of Noah who went forth from the ark were Shem, Ham, and Japheth. (Ham was the father of Canaan.) 19 These three were the sons of Noah, and from these the people of the whole earth were dispersed.* ESV

The Context

Man's wickedness and evil were so great that God was grieved that He had put them on the earth and so He determined to destroy mankind. Only Noah found favor in the eyes of the Lord. The Bible says that Noah was a righteous man and was blameless among all his contemporaries. But the earth was still filled with wickedness *"for all flesh had corrupted their way on the earth."* So God decided to destroy every creature on the earth, including man. But by God's grace He chose to save Noah and his household.

What Do We Know?

In Genesis 7:1 the Lord God spoke to Noah and confirmed that he <u>alone</u> was righteous before the Lord in his generation. However, God allowed Noah's wife, Noah's sons and their wives to enter the ark along with Noah (Gen 7:13). When the flood waters receded, God told Noah and his family to come out of the ark with all the creatures they had saved. Noah's first act was to build an altar and offer burnt sacrifices that were pleasing to God.

God blessed Noah and his sons and made a covenant with Noah, instructing them to be fruitful, multiply, and spread out over the earth – very much like what He told Adam and Eve (Gen 1:28ff).

Observations

Let's agree for our purposes in this study that "grace" means "God's unmerited favor." Grace occurs when someone receives a kindness or blessing from God, not because they earned or deserved it, but because God chose to give it as a gift. New Testament salvation would qualify as the major example of God's grace. Believers chosen by God receive such grace regardless of any worth or merit they may or may not possess.

Another example of God's grace is His deliverance of Israel from slavery in Egypt. But His grace did not end with deliverance. It was expanded by establishing the Jewish nation in the Promised Land. Israel did absolutely nothing to deserve such treatment.

> Deuteronomy 9:5-6   *Not because of your righteousness or the uprightness of your heart are you going in to possess their land, but because of the wickedness of these nations the Lord your God is driving them out from before you, and that he may confirm the word that the Lord swore to your fathers, to Abraham, to Isaac, and to Jacob. 6 "Know, therefore, that the Lord your God is not giving you this good land to possess because of your righteousness, for you are a stubborn people."* ESV

Some define grace as a divine act of love. Describing grace as an action rather than an attitude, probably comes closest to expressing the true meaning of grace. It takes place when someone does something for another out of goodness and love. It is undeserved and there are no strings attached – it is unconditional.

Discussion Questions

A. GENERAL

A1. Eight people were saved on the ark. Were they all equally acceptable to God? [See Gen 6:5; 12, and 7:1.]

> *No, only Noah was acceptable. He was the one who found favor, not his household.
> *Man's wickedness was widespread.
> *Every scheme man's mind thought of was nothing but evil, all the time!
> *The earth and the inhabitants are described as corrupt, both man and beast.
> *NOTE: Noah alone was described as righteous.

A2. List some terms or phrases that you would use to describe the people in Genesis 6:5.
Genesis 6:5   *The Lord saw that the wickedness of man was great in the earth, and that every intention of the thoughts of his heart was only evil continually.* ESV

_____   _____.
_____   _____.
_____   _____.
_____   _____.

> *Possible descriptions: evil, wicked, corrupt, depraved, worthless, inherently immoral, debased, unclean, perverse.

A3. What do you think this verse proves or illustrates about humankind?

> *The inherent evil/wickedness of mankind.
> *Mankind is not inherently good.
> *If man is to have a saving relationship with God, and then

stay in that relationship, all the work must be done by God.
*Man's inherent sinfulness will fight against having a right
relationship with God.
A4. How would you explain Gen 6:6?
Genesis 6:6   *And the Lord was sorry that he had made
man on the earth, and it grieved him to his heart.* ESV

*God was heartbroken and repulsed by mankind's
wickedness.
*God regretted man's sinfulness, not man himself.
*God does not make mistakes.
*God desired a better result.
*Man's depravity was contemptible to God.

A5. Genesis 6:7 tells us how God reacted. How would you react?
What would you have done? Why?
*Genesis 6:7   So the Lord said, "I will blot out man whom I have created
from the face of the land, man and animals and creeping things and birds
of the heavens, for I am sorry that I have made them." ESV*

Q. Is there any indication in this verse that God wants to
"start over"?

*No.

Q. Why would God want to get rid of the animals and
creatures (note 6:12)?

*They were made for man.
*The implication of 6:12 is that "every creature"
had also become corrupt.
*Verse 13 says the earth was filled with evil.

Q. What would you have done?

*Maybe limit the depth of depravity by limiting the
free will of man in some way.
*We have no understanding in order to answer this
question.

A6. How did Noah earn God's favor (6:8)?
>   *It does not say he earned it.
>   *It says he was found to be favorable.
>   *It does not say why exactly . . . except it goes on to describe Noah as righteous and blameless, and that he "walked" with God.

A7. Other than being righteous and blameless, how else is Noah described in 6:9 and what does it mean?
>   *Noah walked with God.
>   *"Walk" implies an intimate relationship.
>   *The figurative sense has decidedly spiritual overtones.
>   *One either walks (conducts his life) as a Christian or as a non-Christian (Rom 8:4; Eph 2:2,10; 1 John 1:6-7).
>   *The believer can walk "in darkness" or "in the light," and is constantly urged to choose the latter.
>   *Only such a path is "worthy of the calling with which you were called" (Eph 4:1).[1 (Nelson's)]

A8. Do you see any significance in the fact that Noah "walked" with God?
>   *Yes, this is likely the primary reason God chose to save Noah.
>   *It means there was a very close, special, and unique relationship.

A9. Who else in the Bible "walked with God"?

>   *ENOCH: Gen 5:22-24 *And after he became the father of Methuselah, Enoch walked with God 300 years and had other sons and daughters. 23Altogether, Enoch lived 365 years. 24 Enoch walked with God; then he was no more, because God took him away* NIV
>   *ABRAHAM and ISAAC: Gen 48:15 *Then he blessed Joseph and said, "May the God before whom my fathers Abraham and Isaac walked, the God who has been my shepherd all my life to this day."* NIV
>   *LEVI: Mal 2:4-6 *"My covenant was with him* [Levi]*, a covenant of life and peace, and I* [God] *gave them to him; this called for reverence and he revered me and stood in awe of my name. 6 True instruction was in his mouth and nothing false was found on his lips. He walked with me in peace and uprightness, and turned many from sin."* NIV

A10. How would you characterize Noah's wife, Noah's sons, and the son's wives, with respect to their nature and status with God?

Their nature:
*Evil, wicked, corrupt, not righteous.

Their standing:
*Blessed. Although they did not find favor with God they received His grace.

Their future:
*They are key players.
*God renews His covenant with both Noah and sons (Gen 9:1, 8).

A11. Why was the family saved? Was it pure arbitrary grace or are there extenuating circumstances?

> *God does nothing that is the result of luck or chance.
> *It is pure grace to provide a support system to the family in the process of repopulating.
> *Because God intended to continue human life on the earth and not start over, He needed to save some females.
> *Grace, but they were fortunate to be related to Noah.

A12. If God wanted to continue human life on the earth and save only Noah, what would be His alternative?

> *Create a new "Eve" for Noah.

> Q. Why is this an alternative God may not have wanted to pursue? What are the potential problems?

> > *Eve was the perfect and compatible wife for Adam and her DNA was already in the line of Noah.
> > *There may be DNA complications we do not understand.
> > *The DNA of the new woman would have to be compatible to Noah and to Eve's DNA inherently in Noah.
> > *Would God make the new woman from Noah's

rib or from the earth? If from Noah, she would have the inherent evil of Noah and all his ancestors.
*Remember, when God made Eve from Adam the two had not yet sinned.
*Unless God made her from Noah, it's possible she wouldn't be truly compatible, like Eve was with Adam.

A13. Why do you think God would change His mind about destroying man because of one righteous man and then save seven others who were not righteous?

> *Grace!
> *God had a plan and a purpose we cannot understand.

A14. What is the significance of the phrase in 7:1 that says Noah was blameless "in this generation"? Genesis 6:9 in Holman says "among his contemporaries" and the NASB says "in his time."

> *Hebrews 11:7 *By faith Noah, being warned by God concerning events as yet unseen, in reverent fear constructed an ark for the saving of his household. By this he condemned the world and became an heir of the righteousness that comes by faith.* ESV
> *Previously there had been righteous and blameless people, but they had all disappeared and the only one righteous in the current generation was Noah.
>
> Q. Why couldn't there be "blameless" people in the son's generation?
>
> > *Because all flesh was corrupt.
>
> Q. Why use the qualifier "in this generation"?
> > *The meaning is not clear or obvious.
> > *Maybe it has no special meaning.
> > *Maybe is simply means "at this time."

A15. These passages make it clear that man was a great disappointment to God. Genesis 6:7 indicates He had decided to destroy man. But one man who found favor with God changed His plans to destroy mankind. Why? What was it about this one man, Noah, that would cause God to change His mind? If Noah was the only good person left, why stop the intended destruction?

>*He saw hope with Noah.
>*Noah was the last of the generations from Adam and Eve who had not been corrupted.
>*Changing His plans might have created difficulties God did not want to pursue.
>*It's possible that Noah was the last who had not been corrupted by the Nephilim (6:1-4).

A16. It is not really Noah who continues the existence of mankind. How would you explain the meaning and impact of Gen 9:19 that indicates it is the three sons who populate the whole earth, not Noah?

>*Whether Noah and his wife have children before or after the flood, their sinful nature is the same, and they would produce children essential the same as their existing family.
>*The only alternative to changing the inherent sinfulness in the human race is a new wife for Noah.
>*However, Noah is still an inherent sinner and as long as his seed is used to repopulate the human race, it will be flawed because of Adam and Eve's original sin.

A17. Why did God save Noah and his wife? They were not used to repopulate the earth.

>*Grace.
>*Noah's character..
>*Noah can influence his children toward righteous behavior after the Flood.
>*Given the length of Noah's life he could have also influenced grandchildren and great-grandchildren as well.

A18. Other than the act of Passover in the Old Testament and Salvation in the New Testament, can you name other significant situations where God extends grace in the Bible?

> *Saul/Paul was saved although he persecuted Christians.
> *Lot's family.
> *Nineveh.
> *Golden Calf – God did not destroy Israel.

> *Q. Can you explain why any of these received God's grace?

>> *No.
>> *God's love is the only explanation!
>> *You can't explain grace!

A19. What does the rainbow represent? Is it a sign to remind people about God's wrath? Is it a sign to remind people about God's grace? Is it a sign to remind people about God's justice? Gen 9:12-15   *This is the sign of the covenant that I make between me and you and every living creature that is with you, for all future generations: 13 I have set my bow in the cloud, and it shall be a sign of the covenant between me and the earth. 14 When I bring clouds over the earth and the bow is seen in the clouds, 15 I will remember my covenant that is between me and you and every living creature of all flesh. And the waters shall never again become a flood to destroy all flesh.* ESV

> *It is a sign of a unilateral covenant between God and man.
> *The covenant is that God will not destroy mankind by a flood again.

> Q. What is the significance of this covenant and the rainbow?

>> *People needed assurance that rain or floods do not mean God is destroying the earth again.
>> *God only promises not to destroy by flood, but He can destroy us by all other means!

A20. What does the story of the Flood tell us about God's patience?

> *His patience will come to an end at some point and man will be judged for his wickedness.

B. APPLICATION

B1. Were you ever given grace by your parents, a teacher, or a boss?

> *Q. What impact did it have on your life?

B2. Have you ever extended grace to someone? What happened?

B3. Do you think God ever sees you as He saw the people in Noah's day?

B4. Would you like to "walk with God"? What do you think that would be like?

B5. The first thing Noah did when he left the ark was build an altar to God. If you were spared some major disaster or calamity in your life, how would you respond?

*Amazing Grace Lyrics

Amazing Grace, how sweet the sound,
That saved a wretch like me.
I once was lost but now am found,
Was blind, but now, I see.

T'was Grace that taught my heart to fear,
And Grace, my fears relieved.
How precious did that Grace appear,
the hour I first believed.

Through many dangers, toils and snares
we have already come.
T'was Grace that brought us safe thus far
and Grace will lead us home.

The Lord has promised good to me,
His word my hope secures.
He will my shield and portion be,
as long as life endures.

When we've been here ten thousand years,
bright shining as the sun.
We've no less days to sing God's praise,
then when we've first begun.

Amazing Grace, how sweet the sound,
That saved a wretch like me.
I once was lost but now am found,
Was blind, but now, I see.

Two Witnesses
during end times

Occurrences of "two witnesses" in Revelation: 2

Theme: End Times

Scripture

Revelation 11:3-13
And I will grant authority to my two witnesses, and they will prophesy for 1,260 days, clothed in sackcloth. 4 These are the two olive trees and the two lampstands that stand before the Lord of the earth. 5 And if anyone would harm them, fire pours from their mouth and consumes their foes. If anyone would harm them, this is how he is doomed to be killed. 6 They have the power to shut the sky, that no rain may fall during the days of their prophesying, and they have power over the waters to turn them into blood and to strike the earth with every kind of plague, as often as they desire. 7 And when they have finished their testimony, the beast that rises from the bottomless pit will make war on them and conquer them and kill them, 8 and their dead bodies will lie in the street of the great city that symbolically is called Sodom and Egypt, where their Lord was crucified. 9 For three and a half days some from the peoples and tribes and languages and nations will gaze at their dead bodies and refuse to let them be placed in a tomb, 10 and those who dwell on the earth will rejoice over them and make merry and exchange presents, because these two prophets had been a torment to those who dwell on the earth. 11 But after the three and a half days a breath of life from God entered them, and they stood up on their feet, and great fear fell on those who saw them. 12 Then they heard a loud voice from heaven saying to them, "Come up here!" And they went up to heaven in a cloud, and their enemies watched them. 13 And at that hour there was a great earthquake, and a tenth of the city fell. Seven thousand people

were killed in the earthquake, and the rest were terrified and gave glory to the God of heaven. ESV

The Context

The Apostle John was both the author and a key character in the book of Revelation. He was the one given the vision, through an angel, concerning "the revelation of Jesus Christ" (Rev 1:1). The angel visited John to tell and show him what would take place in the end times, during a time that has become known as the "tribulation period."

John was shown the wrath of both the Antichrist and God as it is prophesied to occur in the last days. At the time the two witnesses appear, seven seals have already been opened, with the results being described Rev 6. Seven trumpet judgments follow in Rev 8-9. The story of the two witnesses is reported in Rev 11:1-13, between the sixth and seventh trumpet judgments (Rev 11:15). Seven bowl judgments occur after the trumpet judgments. These are described later in Revelation 16.

What Do We Know?

Many find Revelation to be very difficult to interpret and understand. One of the problems is whether to take the story literally or treat it as symbolic.

For this study we will assume a literal interpretation:

> (1) Two real persons witness to the people for 1260 days.
> (2) They have great God-given powers.
> (3) They cannot be killed until their testimony is finished.
> (4) They are killed by the Antichrist and left on the street to decay for 3.5 days.
> (5) They are then raised to life and ascend to heaven.
> (6) A great earthquake kills many.

Observations

In Rev 11:4 John describes the two witnesses as two olive trees and two lampstands "*that stand before the Lord of the earth.*" Revelation 1:20 identifies them as the seven churches. Many scholars also associate the reference to olive trees and lampstands with Zechariah's fifth vision (Zech 4:2-3).

When Zechariah questioned the symbolism of the olive trees and lampstands, the angel explained: "*These are the two anointed ones . . . who stand by the Lord of the whole earth*" (4:14). In Zechariah the two anointed ones were probably Joshua and Zerubbabel, but like many situations in Scripture there may be a double meaning.

It is not clear why John makes this reference in 11:4. Some think it may be to call attention to a major verse familiar to many Christians:

> Zechariah 4:6   *Then he said to me, "This is the word of the Lord to Zerubbabel: Not by might, nor by power, but by my Spirit, says the Lord of hosts."* ESV

In The Book of Revelation (*The Smart Guide to the Bible Series*), Daymond R. Duck and Larry Richards offer another explanation. They also relate 11:4 back to Zech 4:2-6, where the olive trees provide the oil to the lampstands. If the olive oil represents the Holy Spirit, then one could argue that the two witnesses are trees filled with the Holy Spirit. Zech 4:11-15 indicates that the lampstands hold oil and give off light. The two witnesses are the lampstands providing light in an evil world. Thus, each witness becomes an olive tree fueled by the power of the Holy Spirit, bringing light to a dying and wicked world.

This seems like a logical argument, but because the verse is not clear, we can only speculate to its true meaning.

Discussion Questions

A. GENERAL
A1. What are the witnesses going to do (11:3)?

>   *Prophesy.

>   Q. In general, what do they do in 11:5-6?

>>   *Perform miracles (fire; rain; water to blood;
>>   plagues).

A2. What do they do in 11:7?

>   *Proclaim their testimony, probably the gospel and
>   salvation.
>   *Revelation 11:5-7   *And if anyone would harm them, fire
>   pours from their mouth and consumes their foes. If anyone
>   would harm them, this is how he is doomed to be killed. 6
>   They have the power to shut the sky, that no rain may fall
>   during the days of their prophesying, and they have power
>   over the waters to turn them into blood and to strike the
>   earth with every kind of plague, as often as they desire.* ESV

A3. How long are they going to do it (11:3)?

>   *1260 days (3.5 years) to midpoint of tribulation period.
>   *The two witnesses minister during the first half of the
>   tribulation, after which Jerusalem is overrun by the
>   Gentiles for forty-two months (the last half of the
>   tribulation).

A4. What do <u>you</u> think is the purpose or mission of these two
witnesses?

>   *God used the two witnesses to reach and persuade the
>   hearts and minds of unbelieving men and women.
>   Unfortunately many were filled with even greater hatred
>   against God/Christians because of their testimony.
>   *The Gospel could be preached to the whole world by

means of contemporary communication systems.

*Some believe the church will be raptured at the beginning of the Tribulation Period. If this is true these witnesses may be the only source of truth other than the Word of God.

Q. Do you think they accomplished their mission?

>*Yes, God's plans and purposes are never thwarted.
>*Given the hatred expressed at their death, they were obviously effective.
>*The purpose was to give mankind another chance to change their minds through hearing truth.

A5. How are the two witnesses dressed, and what is the significance?

>*Sackcloth, a coarse material that would be uncomfortable.
>Significance: The Old Testament prophets often wore sackcloth when they:

>>*Exhorted Israel for her sin. The two witnesses may be wailing over the sins of God's people (e.g., Joel 1:13).
>>*Mourned for what will happen on and to the earth because people refused to repent and turn to Christ.
>>*Wanted to draw attention to themselves and to their message.
>>*Jeremiah 6:26   *O daughter of my people, put on sackcloth, and roll in ashes; make mourning as for an only son, most bitter lamentation, for suddenly the destroyer will come upon us.* ESV
>>*Joel 1:13   *Put on sackcloth and lament, O priests; wail, O ministers of the altar. Go in, pass the night in sackcloth, O ministers of my God! Because grain offering and drink offering are withheld from the house of your God.* ESV

A6. Why are there two witnesses? What was the significance of two witnesses in Old Testament law (Nu 35:30)?

>*Two was the minimum number of witnesses necessary under Old Testament law (Deut 17:6; 19:15).
>
>*Numbers 35:30   *"If anyone kills a person, the murderer shall be put to death on the evidence of witnesses. But no person shall be put to death on the testimony of one witness."* ESV
>
>**LEADER:** Since these two are resurrected after death, it makes most sense that they are two real people, not symbols for the church, Christian martyrs, Jews/Gentiles, etc. There is no compelling reason to reject the literal story.

A7. Why might God conceal the identity of the two witnesses?

>*Their identity is not important.
>*God does not want us to know who they are.

A8. Many scholars believe that Elijah is one of the two witnesses. Malachi 4:5 gives strong support for that belief. In addition, the ability of the two witnesses to "consume their enemies" with fire (Rev 11:5), points toward Elijah. Can you think of another time when Elijah used the fire of God (see 2 Kings 1:10ff)?

>*2 Kings 1:10   *But Elijah answered the captain of fifty, "If I am a man of God, let fire come down from heaven and consume you and your fifty." Then fire came down from heaven and consumed him and his fifty.* ESV
>
>*On Mt. Carmel, Elijah, in conflict with the prophets of Baal, called down fire on the sacrifice.

>Q. In the Old Testament, what does fire usually symbolize?

>>*Fire implies God's judgment or power at work.
>>*Ps 97:3   *Fire goes before him and burns up his adversaries all around.* ESV
>>*2 Sam 22:9   *Smoke went up from his nostrils, and devouring fire from his mouth; glowing coals flamed forth from him.* ESV

A9. Rev 11:6a provides another hint that one of the witnesses is Elijah. What is the hint? (See also Luke 4:25 and James 5:17.)

> *Drought: Elijah had shut up the heavens in 1 Kings 17.
> *Rev 11:6   *They have the power to shut the sky, that no rain may fall during the days of their prophesying, and they have power over the waters to turn them into blood and to strike the earth with every kind of plague, as often as they desire.* ESV
> *Luke 4:25   *But in truth, I tell you, there were many widows in Israel in the days of Elijah, when the heavens were shut up three years and six months, and a great famine came over all the land.* ESV
> *James 5:17-18   *Elijah was a man with a nature like ours, and he prayed fervently that it might not rain, and for three years and six months it did not rain on the earth.* ESV

> Q. How does Mal 4:5 support Elijah as one of the witnesses?

> > *Mal 4:5 says that Elijah will appear before the great and dreadful day of the Lord comes.

A10. In 11:6 we are also told that the two witnesses have extraordinary power. What can they do?

> *Prevent rain from falling.
> *Turn water into blood.
> *Strike earth with every type of plague.

> Q. Rev 11:6 gives another hint as to the identity of one of the witnesses. Who is it and why?

> > *Plagues: Moses and the Pharaoh, see Ex 7:17-21.
> > *Both Moses and Elijah were involved in the transfiguration (Matt 17:3), which anticipated the second coming.
> > *Matthew 17:3 says Moses and Elijah appeared to them.

A11. What is unique about 11:6c?

>   *As often as <u>they</u> want!
>   *Revelation 11:6   *They have the power to shut the sky, that no rain may fall during the days of their prophesying, and they have power over the waters to turn them into blood and to strike the earth with every kind of plague, as often as they desire.* ESV

>   Q. Is this unprecedented for God?

>>   *I think so. I don't know of any other time that He allowed humans free reign to act in this manner without some restriction.
>>   *It is however, limited to the 1260 days and to the specified powers.

>   Q. Why do you think God gives this authority to the two witnesses?

>>   *God trusted the two witnesses.
>>   *God had more terrible wrath planned later.

A12. Rev 11:7 says they are giving "their testimony." What testimony is that and why does it take 3.5 years?

>   *It's testimony about God rather than their personal testimony.
>   *They are probably quoting Scripture.
>   *They also might be exhorting the Jewish nation, as well as the world in general, to repent and turn to God.

A13. Who is the Beast in 11:7 that kills the two witnesses?

>   *The Antichrist.
>   *The Beast, that is, the Antichrist, is mentioned nine other times in Revelation (13:1; 14:9, 11; 15:2; 16:2; 17:3, 13; 19:20; 20:10).
>   *This is the first reference to "the Beast" in the book of Revelation.

*LEADER: Depending on the nature of your group you may need to define or explain the Antichrist.

*ANTICHRIST: A false prophet and evil being who will set himself up against Christ and the people of God in the last days before the second coming. He stands in opposition to all that Jesus Christ represents (1 John 2:18,22; 4:3; 2 John 7). John wrote that several antichrists existed already in his day (false teachers who denied the deity and the incarnation of Christ) but that the supreme Antichrist of history would appear at some future time. The Antichrist makes war against Christ and His army, but is captured and is "cast alive into the lake of fire burning with brimstone" (Rev 19:20). He is later joined by the devil. The devil, the Beast (or Antichrist), and the False Prophet form a kind of unholy trinity, counterfeiting Father, Son, and Holy Spirit. [2 (Nelsons)]

*NOTE: Satan, the Antichrist, and the false prophet form a false and unholy trinity, counterfeiting the Holy Trinity of Father, Son, and Holy Spirit.

A14. Does the death of the two witnesses make their testimony either more or less reliable?

> *They may lose credibility for 3.5 days, but that all changes with their resurrection!
> *They shed their blood – died for their beliefs.
> *They had finished their testimony. They were indestructible until finished.
> *The bodies of the two were shown disrespect which created a gruesome scene.

A15. Rev 11:8-9 says that their bodies will lie in the street for a period of time. What would that have meant to the people at that time?

> *It was against all rules of human decency as the custom was to treat the dead with care and reverence.
> *Even criminals were buried quickly.
> *It implies great hatred.
> *Ps 79:3   *They have poured out their blood like water all around Jerusalem, and there was no one to bury them.* ESV

A16. What can we conclude about the state of the world from the following references in 11:8-10?

> Sodom: _____.
> *Morality nearly non-existent.
>
> Egypt: _____.
> *Oppression, idolatry, and tyranny: all symbolic of nations that were enemies of God.
>
> Refuse burial:_____.
> *Universal lack of human decency.
>
> Gifts: _____.
> *Celebrating the cessation of God's Word. Their deaths were considered a great victory for the world ruler and Satan. The deaths were celebrated by exchanging gifts – like Christmas!

A17. Rev 11:10 says that these two witnesses tormented or brought judgment to those who lived on the earth. What does that mean? How can that be true?

> *They spoke against the evil Antichrist and the sinful world.
> *God's Word is convicting, and no doubt some were saved by the testimony.
> *Truth will set you free, but it will also convict you of sin.
> *The people heard their testimony over and over again for 3.5 years.
> *It is likely the words were falling on many deaf ears and hard hearts.

A18. Rev 11:11 says that great fear fell on those who saw the two resurrected witnesses. What kind of fear is this? What would the people be thinking?

> *Real fear.
> *Realization that God exists, He has raised the two witnesses to life, and that their resistance is futile.

*Fear that God will pour out His wrath and that all the words of the witnesses are going to come true!
*Some might react in pure terror.
*This is <u>not</u> the "fear of the Lord" that is the beginning of wisdom (Proverbs 1:7).

A19. Rev 12 reports that the people heard God speak to the two witnesses and saw them ascend to heaven in a cloud. What do you suppose the people thought when they experienced this?

*I'm doomed!
*I'm glad that's over. Let's hope they never come back!
*No remorse, no guilt, no desire for the things of God!

A20. What does 11:13 say is the result of all this?

*Revelation 11:13   *And at that hour there was a great earthquake, and a tenth of the city fell. Seven thousand people were killed in the earthquake, and the rest were terrified and gave glory to the God of heaven.* ESV

A21. Were people saved during this time? Why? Why not?

*Very possible some were saved.
*Some may have proclaimed their faith but not from the heart, simply a result of the dramatic events.
*Once all the dust clears most are probably back to hating God for "what He did to them."
*Giving God glory is most likely out of fear and to avoid further judgment, rather than submitting to His Lordship.

B. APPLICATION

B1. How do you think you would respond to all this if you found yourself there?

*I would be searching the Scriptures to determine what's going to happen next and what I should be doing.
*I would try to remember what the two witnesses said I should do.

*If my heart is hard, I'd be more determined to follow the Antichrist.

B2. Do you know anyone who hates Christians? What would it take to break through the barrier of hate and make him/her a believer? Miracles? Empowered preaching? A friend?

B3. Do you know anyone who truly accepted Christ as a result of a major natural disaster? Why do you think that occurred?

The Woman
who rides the Beast

Occurrences of "The Woman" in the Bible: 6-9
(depending on which names or references you include)

Themes: Babylon the Great; Evil; Judgment

---

*<u>LEADER</u>: This lesson is different from all the others in that it could be controversial in certain areas and might be hard for some students to follow. It's a difficult subject. It's also much longer than normal. Depending on your time constraints and your group's knowledge, you may want to spread this lesson over two meetings. We would suggest discussing Section A during the first meeting and Sections B, C, and D in a second meeting.

Scripture

Revelation 17:1-18:3, 18:8
<u>The Great Prostitute and the Beast</u>
17:1 Then one of the seven angels who had the seven bowls came and said to me, "Come, I will show you the judgment of the great prostitute who is seated on many waters, 2 with whom the kings of the earth have committed sexual immorality, and with the wine of whose sexual immorality the dwellers on earth have become drunk." 3 And he carried me away in the Spirit into a wilderness, and I saw a woman sitting on a scarlet Beast that was full of blasphemous names, and it had seven heads and ten horns. 4 The Woman was arrayed in purple and scarlet, and adorned with gold and jewels and pearls, holding in her hand a golden cup full of abominations and the impurities of her sexual immorality. 5 And on her forehead was written a name of mystery:

"Babylon the great,
mother of prostitutes and of earth's abominations."

6 And I saw The Woman, drunk with the blood of the saints, the blood of the martyrs of Jesus. When I saw her, I marveled greatly. 7 But the angel said to me, "Why do you marvel? I will tell you the mystery of The Woman, and of the Beast with seven heads and ten horns that carries her. 8 The Beast that you saw was, and is not, and is about to rise from the bottomless pit and go to destruction. And the dwellers on earth whose names have not been written in the book of life from the foundation of the world will marvel to see the Beast, because it was and is not and is to come. 9 This calls for a mind with wisdom: the seven heads are seven mountains on which The Woman is seated; 10 they are also seven kings, five of whom have fallen, one is, the other has not yet come, and when he does come he must remain only a little while. 11 As for the Beast that was and is not, it is an eighth but it belongs to the seven, and it goes to destruction. 12 And the ten horns that you saw are ten kings who have not yet received royal power, but they are to receive authority as kings for one hour, together with the Beast. 13 These are of one mind and hand over their power and authority to the Beast. 14 They will make war on the Lamb, and the Lamb will conquer them, for he is Lord of lords and King of kings, and those with him are called and chosen and faithful."

15 And the angel said to me, "The waters that you saw, where the prostitute is seated, are peoples and multitudes and nations and languages. 16 And the ten horns that you saw, they and the Beast will hate the prostitute. They will make her desolate and naked, and devour her flesh and burn her up with fire, 17 for God has put it into their hearts to carry out his purpose by being of one mind and handing over their royal power to the Beast, until the words of God are fulfilled. 18 And The Woman that you saw is the great city that has dominion over the kings of the earth."

The Fall of Babylon
18:1 After this I saw another angel coming down from heaven, having great authority, and the earth was made bright with his glory. 2 And he called out with a mighty voice,

"Fallen, fallen is Babylon the great! She has become a dwelling place for demons, a haunt for every unclean spirit, a haunt for every unclean bird, a haunt for every unclean and detestable Beast. 3 For all nations have drunk the wine of the passion of her sexual immorality, and the kings of the earth have committed immorality with her, and the merchants of the earth have grown rich from the power of her luxurious living . . . 8 For this reason her plagues will come in a single day, death and mourning and famine, and she will be burned up with fire; for mighty is the Lord God who has judged her." ESV

The Context

By the end of Revelation 16 all of the seal, trumpet, and bowl judgments have been described and identified. Chapters 17-18 are something like a postscript or additional information related to that which was mentioned earlier:

Revelation 16:19   *The great city was split into three parts, and the cities of the nations fell, and God remembered Babylon the great, to make her drain the cup of the wine of the fury of his wrath.* ESV

Chapters 17 and 18 describe The Woman, the Beast, Babylon, and the scope of their impact on end times events, generally describing God's judgment on Babylon the Great (The Woman).

The first six verses in Chapter 17 describe "The Woman" who is the great or notorious harlot (prostitute). The remainder of the chapter is an interpretation of what John described to his audience in the first six verses. John was "astonished" by what he saw in regard to the "The Woman" and the angel offered to explain the meaning. That explanation follows in the remainder of chapters 17 and 18. Determining who or what is being described as "The Woman," or "Babylon the Great" is key to an accurate understanding of these two chapters.

WARNING: I am <u>not</u> a Bible prophecy expert. I have tried to outline different possible alternative solutions, where desirable, but I have made no attempt to be complete or thorough about explaining everything and going down all the related "rabbit trails." I have tried to make the study interesting enough that it will hold your attention, and provide you with an appreciation for prophecy and some of the possible scenarios for end time events.

What Do We Know?

The most important question has to be, "Who is The Woman?" We learn in 17:5 that The Woman, described as a harlot or notorious prostitute in 17:1, is named the "Mother of Prostitutes." Her actions and nature are further described in the first six verses:

1) She is sitting on many waters (17:1).
2) She is sexually immoral (17:2).
3) She is sitting on a scarlet Beast covered with blasphemous names (17:3).
4) She is dressed in royal colors and adorned with gold and precious jewels (17:4).
5) Her gold cup is filled with everything vile (17:4).
6) Another name on her forehead is "The Mother of the Vile Things of the Earth" (17:5).
7) She is drunk on the blood of the saints (17:6).

The angel, recognizing John's confusion, promised to explain "the mystery of the woman and of the beast" (17:7). That explanation follows in Rev 17:8 – 18:24 in which we learn the following about The Woman:

1) She is sitting on seven mountains that are said to be kings or kingdoms (17:9).
2) The waters on which The Woman is seated (17:1) are peoples and nations (17:15).
3) The ten horns (10 nations) and the Beast will hate the woman and destroy her (17:16).
4) She is described as "the great city" that has influence/control over the kings of the earth (17:18).

5) "Babylon the Great has fallen" (17:16) is declared, confirming that:

> a) All nations and kings were in bed with her (18:3).
> b) The merchants of the earth grew wealthy from her excessive luxury (18:3).

6) God called His people out from her, implying an escape from a nation, city, or kingdom (18:4).
7) She arrogantly "sits as queen," believing she is invincible (18:7).
8) She will be burned with fire, again confirming 17:16 (18:8).

Many believe the "city" to be Rome, and there are significant reasons for this conclusion. Others think it might be the physical Babylon, Jerusalem, or some other future city. Others who associate The Woman with Rome believe that Babylon the Great is the Roman Catholic Church or a world-wide ecumenical religious system. Alternative thought suggests that this "Babylon" is not a real city or place but anywhere Satan rules, like Nazi Germany or Saddam Hussein's Iraq. In this latter interpretation Babylon the Great is not a geographic area but anywhere God is no longer named and wickedness and evil rule in the hearts of man; where each man does as he pleases.

There are arguments for all of the views identified above; some stronger than others. It seems clear from the text that The Woman, "Babylon the Great," is a nation so influential that it controls the commerce of the earth. It is characterized by wealth and excessive luxury and the people do as they see fit, filled with arrogant pride selfishness, unbelief, and unrighteousness.

> Revelation 18:7   *As she glorified herself and lived in luxury, so give her a like measure of torment and mourning, since in her heart she says, "I sit as a queen, I am no widow, and mourning I shall never see."* ESV

A similar example of a harlot appears in the Book of Hosea. That harlot is Gomer's wife, representing the nation of Israel that was unfaithful to God.

> Hosea 4:1-2, 6   *Hear the word of the Lord, O children of Israel, for the Lord has a controversy with the inhabitants of the land. There is no faithfulness or steadfast love, and no knowledge of God in the land; 2 there is swearing, lying, murder, stealing, and committing adultery; they break all bounds, and bloodshed follows bloodshed. . . . 6 My people are destroyed for lack of knowledge; because you have rejected knowledge, I reject you from being a priest to me. . . . ESV*

Luxury and wealth tend to produce pride, and the resulting sense of self sufficiency leads people to believe they do not need God. The result is unfaithfulness, idolatry, injustice, unrighteousness, and a prideful rejection of God. The Woman of Revelation 17 is infected with all these wicked and sinful characteristics. Rev 18:12-14 describes the nation as buying all the goods and cargoes from other nations. Thus, if such a mighty nation stops buying goods from all the other nations, those provider nations now have no major customer and they suffer as well.

> Revelation 18:17, 19   *"For in a single hour all this wealth has been laid waste." And all shipmasters and seafaring men, sailors and all those trade is on the sea, stood far off . . . 19 And they threw dust on their heads as they wept and mourned, crying out, "Alas, alas, for the great city where all who had ships at sea grew rich by her wealth! For in a single hour she has been laid waste." ESV*

A Superpower

What nation or nations could possibly fit the description of a superpower today? We can probably eliminate the Babylon in Iraq, because Jeremiah 50:39-40 says no man will inhabit it. If end times are imminent and will occur in the foreseeable future, the only nation that fits the description as Babylon the Great today is the United States. A superpower nation as described in Rev 17-18 does not come into existence in a short period of time. Several facts about the USA would support the concept of America being Babylon the Great:

- USA is the only present superpower.
- USA's dollar is used everywhere and is the basis for the world's currency.
- USA is the most wealthy nation, living in excessive luxury.
- USA trades with and buys from all nations and we manufacturer much less today.
- USA is so wealthy it can forgive the debts of other nations.

Another argument for America being The Woman is the lack of other mentions of a superpower in any of the key End Times events. Either the USA no longer exists, has been reduced to a minor power because it collapsed economically, or it may be The Woman, Babylon the Great, that is destroyed by fire. Fire typically represents God's judgment and fire could be caused by a bomb, asteroid, or nation-wide terrorist attack.

A possible alternative to the USA would be some conglomeration of nations like the EU or The United Nations. It might be a world system yet to come, but none of these seem to fit like the USA:

- The United States has turned its back on God, trying to eliminate God from every public place.
- The United States is rapidly turning away from the Christian principles on which it was founded.
- The country has and is committing vile atrocities:
    a) Pornography (90% is produced in the USA).
    b) Slavery.
    c) Abortion.
    d) Same-sex marriage.
    e) False teaching.

Thus, the harlot is destroyed:

> Revelation 18:19-21   *And they threw dust on their heads as they wept and mourned, crying out, "Alas, alas, for the great city where all who had ships at sea grew rich by her wealth! For in a single hour she has been laid waste. 20 Rejoice over her, O heaven, and you saints and apostles and prophets, for God has given judgment for you against her!" 21 Then a mighty angel took up a stone like a great*

millstone and threw it into the sea, saying, "So will Babylon the great city be thrown down with violence, and will be found no more;" ESV

The Cup

Rev 17:4 says that The Woman (Babylon the Great) was dressed in royal colors, adorned with precious stones and held a gold cup in her hand filled with the vile adulteries of her prostitution. Those who believe that the USA is The Woman may suggest that the Statue of Liberty is an icon representing the Whore of Babylon. The argument is that the Statue of Liberty is fashioned after the Moon Goddess who was the Queen of Heaven a prostitute. In addition, Liberty (*Libertas*) means the freedom to do what you please. Doing what each one desires or pleases is a very accurate description of our society and where it is heading.

The Statue of Liberty was originally designed with a cup in her hand (like 17:4), but the United States requested that it be changed to a light or lantern, and the French agreed to the change.

Links to historical information about the Statue of Liberty and the eerie likeness to pagan gods can be found on the Internet at:

- *https://www.youtube.com/watch?v=seOsuJw3ucw*
  [rambling voice over of written document below]
- http://humansarefree.com/2014/04/the-secret-worship-of-illuminati-statue.html

ONE WORLD RELIGIOUS SYSTEM

Many believe that the harlot is a one-world religious system begun at the Tower of Babel, located at Old Testament Babylon. Rev 17:6 says that not only does she make others drunk but she herself is drunk – with the blood of the saints. She is involved in the persecution and death of God's people. If this refers to a world-wide ecumenical church, it will not come into existence overnight, but will require the merging of many different religious systems. In this view The Woman represents the false apostate religions that combine into one occult-based religious organization.

The description of this woman as completely evil and vile generally signifies spiritual adultery. The New Testament church is described as a virgin (2 Cor 11:2) and she is warned against spiritual adultery:

> James 4:4   *You adulterous people! Do you not know that friendship with the world is enmity with God? Therefore whoever wishes to be a friend of the world makes himself an enemy of God.* ESV

Apostasy is all around us today. Many churches are filled with false teachers proclaiming false doctrine where the Word of God is skewed to fit the circumstances and the desires of the preacher or teacher:

> 2 Timothy 4:3-4   *For the time is coming when people will not endure sound teaching, but having itching ears they will accumulate for themselves teachers to suit their own passions, 4 and will turn away from listening to the truth and wander off into myths.* ESV

Summary

Thus, The Woman might be:
- The city of Rome.
- Geographical Babylon.
- The city of Jerusalem.
- Some future city.
- The Roman Catholic Church.
- A world-wide ecumenical religious association.
- Not a geographical location, but anywhere Satan rules.
- A superpower nation like the USA.
- Some conglomeration of nations like the European Union.
- A one-world religious system.

Discussion Questions

A. The VISION

A1. In 17:1 The Woman is described as a "notorious prostitute" and in 17:5 she is named the "Mother of Prostitutes." What do these negative terms usually mean when used in Scripture and particularly by an Old Testament prophet?

> *Spiritually unfaithful to the one and only God.
> *Idolatrous.

A2. Rev 17:1 also says The Woman sits on "many waters." How does Rev 17:15 explain the meaning of "waters"? What does this explanation imply?
Revelation 17:15 *And the angel said to me, "The waters that you saw, where the prostitute is seated, are peoples and multitudes and nations and languages." ESV*

> *The waters are peoples, multitudes, nations, and languages.
> *The Woman controls or helps to control the nations.
> *It could refer to a one-world ecumenical religion or as part of some ruling political council with the Antichrist (Beast) as the head and The Woman supporting, partnering, or forcing compliance through economic sanctions, etc.

A3. In 17:2 and 18:3 the term "sexual immorality" is used to describe how other nations ("kings of the earth") interacted with, dealt with, and did business with Babylon. What does that mean? What is the relationship between The Woman and these other nations?
Rev 17:2 *with whom the kings of the earth have committed sexual immorality, and with the wine of whose sexual immorality the dwellers on earth have become drunk. ESV*
Rev 18:3 *"For all nations have drunk the wine of the passion of her sexual immorality, and the kings of the earth have committed immorality with her, and the merchants of the earth have grown rich from the power of her luxurious living." ESV*

*She's at the center of opposition to God and His people.
*She is unfaithful.
*She is demon-possessed.
*She manipulates people through political and religious systems.
*She leads people astray by deceiving through spirits.
*She commits spiritual adultery, betraying the one true God.
*She is immoral in dealings.

A4. Rev 17:2 says the people "became drunk" on the wine of her sexuality. What does that mean?

*The nations so lusted after the result of their immorality that they had no ability to stop (drunk).
*The people of the nations were addicted to her sinful ways.
*They shared in her sinful idolatrous behavior.
*A large number of Christians today may be apostate because their liberal thought has destroyed true belief.

> *NOTE:* Israel's religious adultery is clearly outlined in several Old Testament books and passages. Ezekiel 16 and 23 are prime examples. The book of Hosea relates Hosea's harlot (unfaithful) wife to Israel.

A5. How are The Woman and the Beast described in 17:3-6?

1) She is sitting on a _____ _____.
*scarlet Beast.

2) The Beast is covered with _____ _____.
*blasphemous names.

3) The Beast has seven _____ and ten _____.
*heads   *horns.

4) The colors of The Woman's clothing were _____.
*purple and scarlet.

5) She also wore _____, _____ _____, and _____.
*gold   * precious stones.   *pearls.

6) She had a gold _____ in her hand.
*cup.

7) Her cup was filled with everything vile and with the impurities of her _____.
*prostitution.

8) List the names written on her forehead:

a) _____
*Babylon The Great.

b) _____
*The Mother of Prostitutes.

c) _____
*Mother of Vile Things on the Earth.

9) She is described as being drunk on the:

a) blood of the _____.
*saints.

b) blood of the _____ to Jesus.
*witnesses.

Don't miss the meaning: the saints are being murdered!
*Revelation 17:6   *And I saw The Woman, drunk with the blood of the saints, the blood of the martyrs of Jesus. When I saw her, I marveled greatly.* ESV

A6. Who is the Beast in Rev 17? The "Beast" is mentioned eight times in chapter 17 and is also prominent in Chapter 13:1-8. By what other name or description do we know this character?

Revelation 13:4-8   *And they worshiped the dragon, for he had given his authority to the Beast, and they worshiped the Beast, saying, "Who is like the Beast, and who can fight against it?" 5 And the Beast was given a mouth uttering haughty and blasphemous words, and it was allowed to exercise authority for forty-two months. 6 It opened its mouth to utter blasphemies against God, blaspheming his name and his dwelling, that is, those who dwell in heaven. 7 Also it was allowed to make war on the saints and to conquer them. And authority was given it over every tribe and people and language and nation, 8 and all who dwell on earth will worship it, everyone whose name has not been written before the foundation of the world in the book of life of the Lamb that was slain.* ESV

*The Beast is also known as the Antichrist.

> Q. What do the people do to the Beast (13:4)?
> *Worship him.
>
> Q. What did the Beast do to God (13:6)?
> *Blasphemed His name and dwelling.
>
> Q. What was the Beast given (13:7)?
> *Permission to wage war and conquer the saints.
> *Authority over all the peoples of the earth.
>
> Q. What happens in 13:8?
> *Non-believers worship the Beast.
>
> Q. What is the reason that the people worshipped the Beast (Rev 13:8)?
> *Their names are not in the book of life! (see Rev 20:12, 15). They are not saved. They will not worship Christ. They will not follow God or Christ.
>
> **LEADER:** There are two "Beasts" in Revelation:
>   *Beast from the Sea – Antichrist
>   *Beast from the Land – False Prophet

*There is also a false Trinity:
   *God the Father vs.   Dragon (Satan)
   *Jesus the Son vs.   the Antichrist
   *Holy Spirit vs.   False Prophet

*The comparison is strengthened because the Antichrist recovered from a fatal wound, just as Jesus was resurrected from the dead.

A7. What are the possible explanations or interpretations of The Woman sitting on the Beast?

*Very close relationship, maybe even controlling.
*She participates in oppression and suppression.
*She serves and has a strong influence over the Beast.
*She dominates the Beast.
*The Beast could be jealous of the harlot and her position, status, wealth, or power.
*She could be part of a world council or world body and rules *harshly.* In order to keep her ruling position she must "sit" on them (dominate them).
*She is in partnership with evil world leaders and holds a great deal of influence over the political system headed up by the Beast.

A8. The Woman is described as wearing purple and scarlet, precious jewels, gold, and pearls, and holding a gold cup in her hand. What do you think that implies?

*Flashy, sexy, desirable on the outside.
*Very attractive to those who look only skin deep.
*Wearing royal attire.

Q. What do the contents of the cup tell us?

*Beautiful on the outside (gold) but vile on the inside – her true self.
*Arrogant, proud, and overpowering.

A9. The contents of the cup tell us The Woman is vile on the inside. She is arrogant, proud, and overpowering. If The Woman represents a nation, describe how these characteristics might apply to such a nation.

>   *The nation would be wealthy, powerful, and would say all the right things publically.
>   *It would put on a good outward show for its citizens and the world, but in reality the nation would be untrustworthy, lusting after power and wealth.
>   *No evil would be spared to achieve its goals.
>   *Such a nation would support or destroy world leaders to further its own purposes.

A10. What sins are clearly evident in the following:
Revelation 18:7   *As she glorified herself and lived in luxury, so give her a like measure of torment and mourning, since in her heart she says, "I sit as a queen, I am no widow, and mourning I shall never see."* ESV

>   *Pride.
>   *Living an illusion (unreality).
>   *False sense of security.

A11. One of the mysteries of this passage concerns the names written on The Woman's forehead (17:5). She is identified as "Babylon the Great" and then described by her deeds. What do you think the word "Mother" implies in the last two names: Mother of Prostitutes and Mother of Vile Things of Earth?

>   *She is the "source" of or she "gave birth to" to the sexual immorality and all kinds of evil.
>   *She is the source of or gave birth to immorality, sin, abominations, and indecency.
>   *Evil policies begun in Babylon destroyed some, weakened others, and kept others in poverty.
>   *She is the source or the incubator.

A12. What is The Woman doing in 17:6?

*The Woman was drunk on the blood of the saints.
*She is persecuting and killing Christians. This may include torture and all sorts of atrocities.

B. EXPLANATION of the VISION

In the remainder of chapter 17 the angel explains the meaning of what John saw in the first six verses. In response to John's "great astonishment" he is told the secret meaning of The Woman and the Beast. Note that the language in 17:8 is similar and consistent with Rev 13:4-8 [printed in A6 above].

> Revelation 17:8   *The Beast that you saw was, and is not, and is about to rise from the bottomless pit and go to destruction. And the dwellers on earth whose names have not been written in the book of life from the foundation of the world will marvel to see the Beast, because it was and is not and is to come.* ESV

B1. The Beast is described in 17:8 as coming up from the "abyss." What do you think that means or is intended to imply?

LEADER: this subject is also covered in the Two Witnesses lesson.
*Revelation 11:7   *And when they have finished their testimony, the Beast that rises from the bottomless pit will make war on them and conquer them and kill them.* ESV
*Rev 17:8 may refer back to the first mention of the Beast and his origin (11:7).
*It probably suggests his association with evil, as the abyss was considered to be a deep underground area where evil, demons, etc. resided.
*The Beast, along with the False Prophet, are ultimately thrown into the lake of fire. Satan is put in the abyss for 1000 years before being loosed for a little while, at the end of the 1000 years.

B2. Rev 17:8 confirms the reason that The Woman and the Beast are able to control and influence the people. What is the reason? Explain.

> *Their names are not in the Book of Life, meaning they are inherently evil and enemies of God and will never be saved.
> *They are not of the "elect."
> *Thus, they can be manipulated by a false god who appeals to their own wickedness. See Rev 13:1-8 and Rev 20:12, 15.

B3. Why do you think these non-believers are astonished by the Beast (17:8)? Note the following:
Revelation 13:3
One of its heads seemed to have a mortal wound, but its mortal wound was healed, and the whole earth marveled as they followed the Beast. ESV
Revelation 13:12
It exercises all the authority of the first Beast in its presence, and makes the earth and its inhabitants worship the first Beast, whose mortal wound was healed. ESV

> *He was "killed" and has now come back to life.
> *If you were a non-Christian and saw the leader survive a fatal wound, what would you believe?

B4. Rev 17:9-10 again describes The Woman seated <u>on</u> the seven heads of the Beasts and 17:10 says that these seven heads or mountains are seven kings, meaning that they represent nations. Given The Woman's names, what can you conclude about the nature of these nations?

> *They too are vile, immoral, and evil.
> *They are being influenced by the power of The Woman.

NOTE: The Bible does not identify these seven nations. There are many different views of who they represent. The most widely accepted view seems to be that they represent seven major historical empires: Egypt, Assyria, Babylon, Medo-Persia, Greece, "one that is," and lastly some future empire. But as in all explanations there are some difficulties. Rev 17:10 says that five of the empires have already come and gone. The sixth one currently exists at the time of the writing ("one that is"). If you believe that the reference is to these listed successive empires, then who is the sixth empire? Many believe it is the Roman Empire, the major world power at the time of Jesus.

*LEADER: Many believe that the 7th and future empire is a reestablished Roman Empire.

B5. Rev 17:11-12 describes ten kings who will rule along with the Beast for one hour (a short time). But based on 17:13 who really rules?

> *The Kings give their power and authority to the Beast.
> *The kingdoms probably hate the people or nation that kept them from becoming world leaders themselves. Thus, they hate the Harlot.

B6. Why do you think these kings or nations would turn over their authority to the Beast?

> *The Beast threatens them with destruction.
> *The Beast has the power to accomplish much and kings want to share the success.
> *Life has gotten very difficult and the kings cannot control their people.
> *The Beast can and will use force to bring order and the subordinate king, ruler, or leader wants to avoid blame for the ensuing oppression.

B7. What will the Beast and these kings do while they rule (17:14)?

> *Make war against Jesus (the Lamb).
> * Rev 17:14   *They will make war on the Lamb, and the Lamb will conquer them, for he is Lord of lords and King of kings, and those with him are called and chosen and faithful.* ESV

B8. Rev 17:15 indicates that The Woman's (prostitute's) influence had saturated the "peoples, multitudes, nations, and languages." The text implies that The Woman and the Beast were partners. But something happens to change that relationship. What do 17:16 and 18:8 say occurs?

Rev 17:16   *And the ten horns that you saw, they and the beast will hate the prostitute. They will make her desolate and naked, and devour her flesh and burn her up with fire.* ESV

Rev 18:8   *For this reason her plagues will come in a single day, death and mourning and famine, and she will be burned up with fire; for mighty is the Lord God who has judged her.* ESV

> *Kings (nations) and the Beast hate The Woman (17:16).
> *They turn against her and destroy her with fire (18:8).

B9. Why does all this happen (17:17)?

Revelation 17:17   *For God has put it into their hearts to carry out His plan by having one purpose, and to give their kingdom to the Beast until God's words are accomplished.*

> *God has caused it to happen, in order to carry out His plan and purposes.
> *In these two verses fire may indicate some form of cataclysmic event.
> *Fire could be judgment on the false religion.

C. THE GREAT CITY

The Woman (Babylon The Great) is described as the great city that has control over the kings of the earth (17:18-19). This is a change in perspective as The Woman was not described in these terms earlier in Rev 17. But harlot cities are described elsewhere in Scripture. Nineveh is described as a harlot city in Nahum 3:4. Tyre is described in these terms (Isa 23:16-17), as well as Jerusalem (Eze 16:15ff). The city of Babylon is described as a harlot in Jeremiah 51.

C1. In 18:2 it is reported that Babylon has "fallen" and has become the home for demons and every unclean spirit. Thus, the entity represented by the term "Babylon the Great" is the source of spiritual and moral indecency and is described as "unclean" and "despicable."

> Q. How will Babylon be judged (18:6a)?

> *Paid back double for what she has done.

C2. Kings, merchants, and seamen are all listed as mourning or standing far off. This section is similar to the lament for Tyre in Ezekiel 27. Many of the goods listed in 18:12-13 are also listed in Ezekiel 27, where it is also said that those who trade among the peoples will become an object of horror and will never exist again (27:36). This is also described in Rev 18:9-24.

18:9 Kings (nations) will commit sexual immorality with Babylon and will mourn at her _____. *burning.

18:11 Merchants will mourn because The Woman is no longer able to buy their _____. *merchandise.

18:13 The merchandise includes slaves and human _____. *lives.

18:17 In a single hour the wealth will be _____. *destroyed.

18:17 Sea captains and sailors will also stand _____. *far off.

18:21 Babylon will never be found _____. *again.

18:22-23 Nothing will be heard in Babylon _____. *again.

18:23 All this happened because the nations were deceived by Babylon's _____. *sorcery

NOTE: Some think that "the great city" is the geographical city of Babylon. If that is the case, then the end time is not close at hand. This type of world-wide influence, power, trade, and dominant economic influence does not happen overnight. Therefore, those who believe that end times are imminent will find that the geographical Babylon makes no logical sense.

C3. What are the kinds of things that a decadent nation becomes "drunk" on?

>   *Power.
>   *Pride.
>   *Violence.
>   *Wealth.
>   *False gods.

*Drugs.
*Sexual immorality.
*Freedom to do anything they please ("liberty").

C4. The nature of the destruction of Babylon is mentioned in 18:10, 17, and 19. What is the common thread in these three verses?

>*The destruction will occur in "<u>one hour</u>!"
>*It is possible that this simply means a "<u>short time</u>. It could refer to the seven-year tribulation period because Rev 3:10 refers to being saved from the hour of testing.
>*It is also possible that it literally means <u>60 minutes</u>, or a similarly <u>short time</u>.
>*In 18:8 it says that her plagues will come in <u>one day</u>.

>*Q. How could all this happen?

>>*Atomic or nuclear explosion.
>>*Asteroid.
>>*Terrorists acts that blow up gas/oil lines and refineries destroying infra-structure.
>>*Note that 18:15, 17 it says they stand far off because of pollution (maybe radiation) from the real fire.

D. APPLICATION

D1. Given all you have read and understand about Babylon the Great, what do you think <u>you</u> are called to <u>do</u> next?

>*Pray.
>*Evangelize.
>*But do not be fearful.

D2. Many who believe in the pre-tribulation rapture of the Church respond to end times studies with little interest because they think they will not be on earth to experience any of the events described in Revelation. Others find the text and strange descriptions too difficult to understand in a real life scenario. But Rev 1:3 gives us a unique perspective about the Book of Revelation. What is it?

Revelation 1:3   *Blessed is he who reads and those who hear the words of this prophecy, and keep those things which are written in it; for the time is near.* NKJV

> Q. How could this be true? What does this mean to you?

>> *Peace: I know who wins
>> *Satisfaction: I know evil will fail and ultimately be punished and destroyed.

24 Elders
in the throne room

Occurrences of "24 elders" in the Bible: 5

Themes: Worship

Scripture

Revelation 4:4, 9-11　　The Throne Room in Heaven
Around the throne were twenty-four thrones, and seated on the thrones were twenty-four elders, clothed in white garments, with golden crowns on their heads. . . . 9 And whenever the living creatures give glory and honor and thanks to him who is seated on the throne, who lives forever and ever, 10 the twenty-four elders fall down before him who is seated on the throne and worship him who lives forever and ever. They cast their crowns before the throne, saying, 11 "Worthy are you, our Lord and God, to receive glory and honor and power, for you created all things, and by your will they existed and were created." ESV

Revelation 5:5-8, 13-14　　Worthy to Open Scroll
And one of the elders said to me, "Weep no more; behold, the Lion of the tribe of Judah, the Root of David, has conquered, so that he can open the scroll and its seven seals." 6 And between the throne and the four living creatures and among the elders I saw a Lamb standing, as though it had been slain, with seven horns and with seven eyes, which are the seven spirits of God sent out into all the earth. 7 And he went and took the scroll from the right hand of him who was seated on the throne. 8 And when he had taken the scroll, the four living creatures and the twenty-four elders fell down before the Lamb, each holding a harp, and golden bowls full of incense, which are the prayers of the saints. . . . 13 And I heard every creature in heaven and on earth and under the earth and in the sea,

and all that is in them, saying, "To him who sits on the throne and to the Lamb be blessing and honor and glory and might forever and ever!" 14 And the four living creatures said, "Amen!" and the elders fell down and worshiped. ESV

Revelation 7:11-12   Elders with the Great Multitude
And all the angels were standing around the throne and around the elders and the four living creatures, and they fell on their faces before the throne and worshiped God, 12 saying, "Amen! Blessing and glory and wisdom and thanksgiving and honor and power and might be to our God forever and ever! Amen." ESV

Revelation 11:15-17   The Seventh Trumpet
Then the seventh angel blew his trumpet, and there were loud voices in heaven, saying, "The kingdom of the world has become the kingdom of our Lord and of his Christ, and he shall reign forever and ever." 16 And the twenty-four elders who sit on their thrones before God fell on their faces and worshiped God, 17 saying, "We give thanks to you, Lord God Almighty, who is and who was, for you have taken your great power and begun to reign." ESV

Revelation 19:4-5, 10   Hallelujah!
And the twenty-four elders and the four living creatures fell down and worshiped God who was seated on the throne, saying, "Amen. Hallelujah!" 5 And from the throne came a voice saying, "Praise our God, all you his servants, you who fear him, small and great." . . . 10 Then I fell down at his feet to worship him, but he said to me, "You must not do that! I am a fellow servant with you and your brothers who hold to the testimony of Jesus. Worship God." For the testimony of Jesus is the spirit of prophecy. ESV

The Context

The 24 elders are mentioned only in the book of Revelation and in every instance they are worshipping God. In every situation the text reports that the elders fell down to worship. In each case they are in the throne room of God in the presence of the Almighty.

We do not know for sure who these 24 elders are. They may be the leadership of the faith in the Old and New Testaments, that is the sons of Jacob, representing the twelve tribes of Israel, plus the twelve Apostles. Or they might represent the body of Christ, just as the 24 priests in 1 Chronicles 24 represented the people. But discovering who they represent is less important than understanding what they are doing.

What Do We Know?

In Rev 4:11 the 24 elders tell us why they worship: because God is worthy and because He is the Creator and sustainer of all things.

In 5:8 John confirms that Jesus is alive and in the throne room with God, the Father. Each of the 24 elders holds a harp and a golden bowl filled with incense which are identified as the prayers of the saints. The saints are not the outstanding leaders of the faith, as one might expect, but rather the ordinary believer: so these are your prayers and mine! It is not clear why each elder has a harp. One can only assume it is to assist in the worship since in 5:9 it says they are singing a new song.

In 5:13 we may see the possible fulfillment of Php 2:10:11 which indicates that every knee will bow and every tongue confess that Jesus is Lord. Nothing is said about bowing, but "all creatures" (dead and alive) are acknowledging the Lamb of God, the Lord Jesus Christ!

The phrase in 19:10, "the testimony about Jesus is the spirit of prophecy," probably means that the entire Bible, which is a testimony and prophecy about Jesus, is true. Jesus is at the center of all prophecy and God's Word testifies about Him.

Implications and Observations

Worship is a function that will never end because God is eternal and has no end. Evangelism will ultimately cease but the worship of our God and Savior will be eternal. Therefore, if we have one practice we want to learn while we are still here on earth preparing for eternity, it should be that we worship in spirit and in truth and not in vain.

Worship that is unacceptable to God cannot be allowed in our life.

Discussion Questions

<u>A. GENERAL</u>

A1. What are the 24 elders wearing in Rev 4:4?

*White clothes.

A2. Who else in the book of Revelation is dressed in similar clothing?

3:4 _____
*Those in Sardis who have "not soiled their clothes."
*They are worthy.

3:5 _____
*He who overcomes.

3:18 _____
*Those in Laodicea who buy gold refined in the fire and white clothes to cover their shameful wickedness.

6:11 _____
*Those in heaven under the altar after 5th seal
*They were slain because of the Word of God and their testimony.

7:9 _____
*The great multitude in heaven after the 144,000 are sealed from the 12 tribes of Israel.

19:14 _____
*The armies of heaven. These are angelic beings (Dt 33:2; Ps 68:17) or believers (Rev 17:14)
*Rev 17:14 *They will make war on the Lamb, and the Lamb will conquer them, for he is Lord of lords and King of kings, and those with him are called and chosen and faithful.* ESV

*Note: If 17:14 describes those in 19:14, these are believers, since angels would not be described as called, chosen, or faithful.

A3. In general, how would you characterize these groups that are dressed in white?

*Believers.
*Overcomers.
*Truly committed Christ-followers.

A4. How did the robes of the "great multitude" become white (7:14)?

*Washed in the blood of the Lamb.
LEADER: You may want to discuss the "great multitude" in Rev 7:14-17 with the group. Who are they?
*Rev 7:14-17   *I said to him, "Sir, you know." And he said to me, "These are the ones coming out of the great tribulation. They have washed their robes and made them white in the blood of the Lamb. 15 Therefore they are before the throne of God, and serve him day and night in his temple; and he who sits on the throne will shelter them with his presence. 16 They shall hunger no more, neither thirst anymore; the sun shall not strike them, nor any scorching heat. 17 For the Lamb in the midst of the throne will be their shepherd, and he will guide them to springs of living water, and God will wipe away every tear from their eyes." ESV*

A5. What does "*washed in the blood of the Lamb*" mean?

*Their sins are covered by the atoning death of Christ.
LEADER: It doesn't matter for our purposes whether this multitude is all believers or just the believers martyred during the Tribulation.

A6. What would you say is the significance of the "white clothes"?

*Pure.
*Blessed.
*Covered by Christ.
*A member of Christ's followers.
*An overcomer.
*Represents God and God's people.

A7. What did the 24 elders have on their heads?

> *Gold crowns.

A8. Why gold crowns? Based on Rev 3:21, what do you think these crowns represent?
Revelation 3:21   *The one who conquers, I will grant him to sit with me on my throne, as I also conquered and sat down with my Father on his throne.* ESV

> *Victory.
> *Royal calling to the reign of Christ.
> *Remember, they represent rewards, not salvation!

> Q. What do <u>you</u> think it means that someone would sit with Jesus on His throne?

>> *Part of the family of the King.
>> *Possess authority to help rule (at least partially).

> Q. What further do we learn in Rev 22:5?

>> *Rev 22:5 *". . . they will reign forever and ever."*

A9. Why would the 24 elders throw their crowns on the floor?

> *They are giving them back to God, from whom they received them.
> *Because of the grace of God.
> *Received them because of the power of God in their lives.
> *They understand they do not deserve the crowns.
> *Only God is worthy to wear a crown.
> *It's an act of submission.
> *Meaning: Acknowledgement of God as Creator and Redeemer. He deserves all our praise and worship.
> *Casting Crowns: We are not worthy to wear a gold crown in the presence of Almighty God, since
>> (1) He is the King,
>> (2) He is perfect, and
>> (3) He is worthy.

*Anything we did that deserves notice was done through the power of the Holy Spirit.

A10. What do the following verses tell us about crowns?

(A) _____

_____

Revelation 2:10   *Do not fear what you are about to suffer. Behold, the devil is about to throw some of you into prison, that you may be tested, and for ten days you will have tribulation. Be faithful unto death, and I will give you the crown of life.* ESV

*Be faithful and Christ will give you the crown of life.
*Eternal life is the reward for being faithful.
*Eternal life is the wreath awarded for winning the race.

(B) _____

_____

Revelation 3:11   *I am coming soon. Hold fast what you have, so that no one may seize your crown.* ESV

*Hold on.
*Stand firm.
*Don't give up – so no one will take your crown.

Q. Who could take your crown? Who would want to take your crown?

*Satan: He does not want you to be successful.
*Self: No longer deserve it because of sin.

(C) _____

_____

Revelation 14:14   *Then I looked, and behold, a white cloud, and seated on the cloud one like a son of man, with a golden crown on his head, and a sharp sickle in his hand.* ESV

*Jesus (one like a the son of man) is wearing a crown of gold.
*Victory wreath.

(D) _____

_____

Revelation 19:12   *His eyes are like a flame of fire, and on his head are many diadems, and he has a name written that no one knows but himself.* ESV

>   *Rider on the white horse (Jesus) wearing many diadems (crowns).
>   Q. What do you think these "many crowns" represent?
>
>   >   *The right to rule.
>   >   *He is the King of kings.
>   >   *Note: Crowns on usurpers:
>   >   *Revelation 12:3   *And another sign appeared in heaven: behold, a great red dragon, with seven heads and ten horns, and on his heads seven diadems.* ESV

A11. What do we learn about crowns in the following? How are they earned? What are they for?

(A) _____

_____

2 Tim 4:8   *Henceforth there is laid up for me the crown of righteousness, which the Lord, the righteous judge, will award to me on that Day, and not only to me but also to all who have loved his appearing.* ESV

>   *Crown of Righteousness:
>   *May refer to the righteous state of believers.
>   *A crown consisting of righteousness.
>   *"That Day" refers to the Second Coming.
>   *"All who have loved His appearing" refers to believers.

(B) _____

_____

1 Corinthians 9:25-26   *Every athlete exercises self-control in all things. They do it to receive a perishable wreath, but we an imperishable. 26 So I do not run aimlessly; I do not box as one beating the air.* ESV
>   *A crown that will last forever; it is eternal.

(C) _____

_____

James 1:12   *Blessed is the man who remains steadfast under trial, for when he has stood the test he will receive the crown of life, which God has promised to those who love him.* ESV
>   *The crown of life for enduring trials.
>   Q. Who gets this crown?

>>   *One who remains steadfast under trial.
>>   *One who loves God.

(D) _____

_____

1 Peter 5:4   *And when the chief Shepherd appears, you will receive the unfading crown of glory.* ESV

>   *Crown of glory

A12. What do the elders do in 5:8; 5:14; 7:11; 11:16; 19:4?

>   *Fell down and worshipped.

>   Q. What do you think is the significance of the elders' prostrating themselves?

>>   *Falling down in worship was common in those days.
>>   *It was a sign of submission.
>>   *It was an act of deference.
>>   *Recognition that He is the sovereign God.

A13. What does John do in 19:10 and 22:8-9 and what is he told by the angel?

>   *John falls at the angel's feet and worships.
>   *The angel says not to worship him.
>   *Revelation 22:9   . . . *"You must not do that! I am a fellow servant with you and your brothers the prophets, and with those who keep the words of this book. Worship God."* ESV

B. WORSHIP

B1. Write out a definition of worship. You can find various definitions in many sources. Choose the best parts of what you find and write your definition below:

> *Worship is the ceremony or response we employ to express our devotion, allegiance, and honor to God.
> *Worship can be the acknowledgment or demonstration of His presence, nature, ways, or works.
> *It can be inward, such as love, joy, and trust.
> *It can be outward, such as service, prayer, posture, praise, singing, or giving.

> ***LEADER**: Consider asking the participants to submit their definitions in advance by email and you consolidate them into one document to distribute and possibly discuss during your meeting.

B2. What do you think is the most important issue regarding the subject of worship? (e.g what, where, when, who, how) Explain.

> *Who you worship is more important than where, when, and how.

> ***LEADER**: After the discussion, read Exodus 20:2-8 and ask your group for their reactions to this passage.
> *Exodus 20:2-8
> *2 I am the Lord your God, . . .*
> *3 You shall have no other gods before me.*
> *4 You shall not make for yourself a carved image, or any likeness of anything . . .*
> *5 You shall not bow down to them or serve them [idols], for I the Lord your God am a jealous God . . .*
> *6 . . . showing steadfast love to . . . those who love me . . .*
> *7 You shall not take the name of the Lord your God in vain . . .*
> *8 Remember the Sabbath day, to keep it holy. . . .* ESV

B3. How might you relate the Great Commandment to worship?
Mark 12:30 *And you shall love the Lord your God with all your heart and with all your soul and with all your mind and with all your strength.* ESV

    *Worship is the top priority.

    ***LEADER:** You might ask your group, "Does anyone believe the most important relational response to God is something other than worship?"
    *Worship is the natural result of loving God with all our heart, mind, body, and soul!

B4. Do you think that in order to truly worship we must "fall on our knees"?

    *No, that was the custom in those days however, kneeling before God is still a reverent act of submission.
    *Worship is not a function of what we do, but who we worship with the whole heart.

B5. What are the four conditions in Hebrews 10:22 that describe how we draw near to God?
Hebrews 10:19-22 *Therefore, brothers, since we have confidence to enter the Most Holy Place by the blood of Jesus, 20 by a new and living way opened for us through the curtain, that is, his body, 21 and since we have a great priest over the house of God, 22 let us draw near to God with a <u>sincere heart</u> in <u>full assurance of faith</u>, having our <u>hearts sprinkled to cleanse us from a guilty conscience</u> and having our <u>bodies washed with pure water</u>.* NIV

*<u>"sincere heart"</u>
    *Undivided allegiance to God in our inner being.
    *It is the "pure in heart" who will see God.
* <u>"full assurance of faith"</u>
    *Faith that knows no hesitation.
    *Fully trusting in God.
*<u>"hearts sprinkled . . . from a guilty conscience"</u>
    *No wavering. Our guilt is washed away.
    *Based on His sacrifice we are spiritually cleansed.
*<u>"bodies washed with pure water"</u>

*Inner cleansing rather than empty ceremony.

*Ezekiel 36:25   *I will sprinkle clean water on you, and you will be clean; I will cleanse you from all your impurities and from all your idols.* NIV

B6. Choose <u>one</u> of the conditions above and write a sentence or two describing what that condition means.

B7. Based on the following, what are the requirements for worship?

a. Our worship must be _____.

Heb 12:28-29   Therefore let us be grateful for receiving a kingdom that cannot be shaken, and thus let us offer to God acceptable worship, with reverence and awe, 29 for our God is a consuming fire. ESV

* right / acceptable

b. We must come to worship God with or through _____.

John 14:6   *Jesus said to him, "I am the way, and the truth, and the life. No one comes to the Father except through me.* ESV

*Christ

c. The first thing we must do in approaching a holy God is to be free of _____ .

Hebrews 10:4   For it is impossible for the blood of bulls and goats to take away sins. ESV

*Sin.

d. We must approach God in worship with _____ _____
and a _____ _____.

Psalms 24:3-4   *Who shall ascend the hill of the Lord? And who shall stand in his holy place? 4 He who has clean hands and a pure heart, who does not lift up his soul to what is false and does not swear deceitfully. ESV*

   *Clean hands and a pure heart.

e. My entire _____ is an act of worship.

Romans 12:1   *I appeal to you therefore, brothers, by the mercies of God, to present your bodies as a living sacrifice, holy and acceptable to God, which is your spiritual worship. ESV*

   *Life.

f. Our worship must be rooted in God's _____.

Ephesians 5:26   *that he might sanctify her, having cleansed her by the washing of water with the word, ESV*

   *Word.

B8. Based on the following verses what kind of worship must we avoid?

a. _____

John 4:22   *You worship what you do not know; we worship what we know, for salvation is from the Jews. ESV*

   *Ignorant – what we do not know.
   *Worship based on something other than the truth of God's Word.

b. _____

Romans 1:22-23   *Claiming to be wise, they became fools, 23 and exchanged the glory of the immortal God for images resembling mortal man and birds and animals and reptiles. ESV*

   *Improper.
   *Idolatrous.

c. _____

Mal 1:8   *When you bring blind animals for sacrifice, is that not wrong? When you sacrifice crippled or diseased animals, is that not wrong?*

* Inferior – God wants the best.
*Having no real value.
*Marked by futility.
*No purpose.
*Trying to cheat God.

d. _____

Matthew 15:9 *in vain do they worship me, teaching as doctrines the commandments of men.* ESV

*Teaching based on something other than the Word.
*Result is "in vain."

Q. What does worshiping "in vain" mean?

*Worthless or useless.
*Of no purpose.
*A waste.

B9. What are your conclusions after studying and thinking about this subject?

*Worship is SERIOUS business.
*There are important things to do and things not to do.
***NOTE TO LEADER**: Impress on the group the seriousness of worship.

C. APPLICATION

D1. PREPARED: Do I come to worship prepared with clean hands and a pure heart? (Ps 24:3-4)

a. Am I repentant and forgiven? Do I come to worship clean, and free from sin?
b. Have I read or studied the scripture in advance?
c. Have I bathed my life and my worship in prayer?

D2. HEART: Do I come to worship with the right heart attitude?

> a. Do I come to worship humble and with a contrite heart (surrendered and submissive)?
> b. Have I substituted rites, ceremonies, and activity for true heartfelt worship?

D3. FOCUS: Is the Lord Jesus Christ my primary focus, the number one priority of my life?

> a. Is Jesus constantly before me?
> b. Is He foremost in my thoughts?
> c. Is my life God-centered?

D4. LIVING SACRIFICE: Is my life a living sacrifice unto God? (Ro 12:1)

> a. Have I submitted my life to Christ?
> b. Have I laid my crowns at His feet, like the 24 elders?

D5. SABBATH: Am I honoring and keeping "the Sabbath" [Sunday] holy?

> a. Is Sunday special in my life or is it like any other day?

D6. UNACCEPTABLE: Am I doing anything in worship that is unacceptable to God?

> a. Is my worship ignorant, improper, inferior, in vain, false, without repentance, or not from heart?
> b. Is my worship in conflict with His Word?

New Jerusalem
at end of millennium

Occurrences of "new Jerusalem" in the Bible: 2

Theme: Eternity

Scripture

Revelation 21:1-8

Then I saw a new heaven and a new earth, for the first heaven and the first earth had passed away, and the sea was no more. 2 And I saw the holy city, new Jerusalem, coming down out of heaven from God, prepared as a bride adorned for her husband. 3 And I heard a loud voice from the throne saying, "Behold, the dwelling place of God is with man. He will dwell with them, and they will be his people, and God himself will be with them as their God. 4 He will wipe away every tear from their eyes, and death shall be no more, neither shall there be mourning nor crying nor pain anymore, for the former things have passed away."

5 And he who was seated on the throne said, "Behold, I am making all things new." Also he said, "Write this down, for these words are trustworthy and true." 6 And he said to me, "It is done! I am the Alpha and the Omega, the beginning and the end. To the thirsty I will give from the spring of the water of life without payment. 7 The one who conquers will have this heritage, and I will be his God and he will be my son. 8 But as for the cowardly, the faithless, the detestable, as for murderers, the sexually immoral, sorcerers, idolaters, and all liars, their portion will be in the lake that burns with fire and sulfur, which is the second death." ESV

Revelation 21:22-27
And I saw no temple in the city, for its temple is the Lord God the Almighty and the Lamb. 23 And the city has no need of sun or moon to shine on it, for the glory of God gives it light, and its lamp is the Lamb. 24 By its light will the nations walk, and the kings of the earth will bring their glory into it, 25 and its gates will never be shut by day—and there will be no night there. 26 They will bring into it the glory and the honor of the nations. 27 But nothing unclean will ever enter it, nor anyone who does what is detestable or false, but only those who are written in the Lamb's Book of Life. ESV

Revelation 22:1-5
Then the angel showed me the river of the water of life, bright as crystal, flowing from the throne of God and of the Lamb 2 through the middle of the street of the city; also, on either side of the river, the tree of life with its twelve kinds of fruit, yielding its fruit each month. The leaves of the tree were for the healing of the nations. 3 No longer will there be anything accursed, but the throne of God and of the Lamb will be in it, and his servants will worship him. 4 They will see his face, and his name will be on their foreheads. 5 And night will be no more. They will need no light of lamp or sun, for the Lord God will be their light, and they will reign forever and ever. ESV

Revelation 22:12-16
"Behold, I am coming soon, bringing my recompense with me, to repay everyone for what he has done. 13 I am the Alpha and the Omega, the first and the last, the beginning and the end." 14 Blessed are those who wash their robes, so that they may have the right to the tree of life and that they may enter the city by the gates. 15 Outside are the dogs and sorcerers and the sexually immoral and murderers and idolaters, and everyone who loves and practices falsehood. 16 "I, Jesus, have sent my angel to testify to you about these things for the churches. I am the root and the descendant of David, the bright morning star." ESV

The Context

Rev 21:1 reports that there is a new heaven and new earth and John describes this new environment as best he can. These last two chapters of the Bible provide a brief look at life at the end of the millennium, as the people of God are about to enter into eternity. Evil has been destroyed by God's wrath, Satan has been thrown into the lake of fire, and death has been eradicated from creation. Life is about to return to days similar to those at the beginning in the Garden of Eden. The angel is continuing to show John (the author) wonders beyond his imagination. Revelation 22:3 sums it all up:

> *No longer will there be anything accursed, but the throne of God and of the Lamb will be in it, and his servants will worship him.* ESV

What Do We Know?

Chapter 20 of Revelation reports the cataclysmic events at the great white throne judgment: death, Hades, and anyone not in the Book of Life are thrown into the lake of fire. At the end of the millennium Satan is released from the abyss for a short time (20:1-4). Satan deceives some of the people living on earth and gathers them together to surround the camp of God's people:

> Revelation 20:9-10   *And they marched up over the broad plain of the earth and surrounded the camp of the saints and the beloved city, but fire came down from heaven and consumed them, 10 and the devil who had deceived them was thrown into the lake of fire and sulfur where the beast and the false prophet were, and they will be tormented day and night forever and ever.* ESV

At that point John reports that he saw a great white throne where people were being judged.

> Revelation 20:14-15   *Then Death and Hades were thrown into the lake of fire. This is the second death, the lake of fire. 15 And if anyone's name was not found written in the book of life, he was thrown into the lake of fire.* ESV

It is my understanding based on the timelines of the other resurrections and judgments that the only ones not yet judged at this point in time are the dead unsaved non-believers. Their names are not in the Book of Life and they all are thrown into the lake of fire.

But then John saw a new heaven and a new earth!

Discussion Questions

A. REVELATION 21

A1.   What do we know about the new environment?
Revelation 21:1   *Then I saw a new heaven and a new earth, for the first heaven and the first earth had passed away, and the sea was no more. ESV*

> *The old heaven and earth are gone ("passed away").
> *There is no sea.
>
> Q. What additional information is supplied by Isa 65:17?
> Isaiah 65:17   *For behold, I create new heavens and a new earth, and the former things shall not be remembered or come into mind. ESV*
>
> > *The past will not be remembered.
>
> Q. Is this fact significant?
>
> > *Yes. The sin, sadness, and depravity of the past will be forgotten.
> > *Former friends or loved ones who are not with you will not be remembered.

A2. What do we learn about the new Jerusalem?
Revelation 21:2   *And I saw the holy city, new Jerusalem, coming down out of heaven from God, prepared as a bride adorned for her husband. ESV*

*It is comes down from heaven. Also see 21:10.
*It is from God.
*It has been prepared (beautifully) for its new residents.

*LEADER: You might explain the nature of the marriage process in Jesus' day. It began with a betrothal, which was a legal contract requiring a divorce to dissolve. During this period, the bride and groom lived separately while the groom prepared their future home, usually an addition onto his parent's home. When the groom had everything prepared he went to get his bride and the wedding took place.

A3. What do we learn about the residents of the city?
Revelation 21:3   *And I heard a loud voice from the throne saying, "Behold, the dwelling place of God is with man. He will dwell with them, and they will be his people, and God himself will be with them as their God."* ESV

*God will live with His people in the city.

Q. What do you think that means? How do you visualize God living among us?

*Unimaginable – we have no clue.
*Peace, rest, no fear, no disease no conflict.
*Surrounded by His glory.

Q. What is said about God's relationship with the residents of the city?

*They will be His people.
*He will be their God.
*Therefore, it is a two-way relationship.
*He will be our God: Gen 17:8; Ex 29:45; Jer 31:33; Eze 11:20; 2 Cor 6:16; Heb 8:10.

A4. What further do we learn about life in the New Jerusalem?
Rev 21:4   *He will wipe away every tear from their eyes, and death shall be no more, neither shall there be mourning nor crying nor pain anymore, for the former things have passed away.* ESV

> *No tears and no death.
> *No mourning, crying, or pain.
> *Leviticus 26:11-12   *I will make my dwelling among you, and my soul shall not abhor you. 12 And I will walk among you and will be your God, and you shall be my people.* ESV

A5. The text says that one must be the "victor" or "overcome" in order to inherit all this. What do you think that means?
Revelation 21:7   *The one who conquers will have this heritage, and I will be his God and he will be my son.* ESV

> *Stand firm.
> *John 16:33   *I have said these things to you, that in me you may have peace. In the world you will have tribulation. But take heart; I have overcome the world.* ESV [Assurance]
> *1 John 4:4   *Little children, you are from God and have overcome them, for he who is in you is greater than he who is in the world.* ESV   [Holy Spirit]

> Q. What does it mean to be an overcomer? Who is an overcomer?

>> *1 John 5:4   *For everyone who has been born of God overcomes the world. And this is the victory that has overcome the world — our faith.* ESV

A6. What does Revelation 2 and 3 promise to the overcomer?

> 2:7_____
> Rev 2:7   *He who has an ear, let him hear what the Spirit says to the churches. To the one who conquers I will grant to eat of the tree of life, which is in the paradise of God.* ESV
> *The right to eat from the tree of life.

2:11_____

<u>Rev 2:11</u> *He who has an ear, let him hear what the Spirit says to the churches. The one who conquers will not be hurt by the second death.* ESV

   *Not hurt by the second death (also see 21:8).

2:17_____

<u>Rev 2:17</u> *He who has an ear, let him hear what the Spirit says to the churches. To the one who conquers I will give some of the hidden manna, and I will give him a white stone, with a new name written on the stone that no one knows except the one who receives it.* ESV

   *White stone: Often served as a "ticket" to an event.
   *Manna: Food from Heaven, or spiritual food.
   *Secret name: Exclusively between you and God.

2:26-29_____

<u>Rev 2:26-29</u>   *The one who conquers and who keeps my works until the end, to him I will give authority over the nations, 27 and he will rule them with a rod of iron, as when earthen pots are broken in pieces, even as I myself have received authority from my Father. 28 And I will give him the morning star. 29 He who has an ear, let him hear what the Spirit says to the churches.* ESV

   *Authority over nations.
   *Bright morning star. Jesus is the morning star.
   *Revelation 22:16   *"I, Jesus, have sent my angel to testify to you about these things for the churches. I am the root and the descendant of David, the bright morning star."* ESV
   *Numbers 24:17   *I see him, but not now; I behold him, but not near: a star shall come out of Jacob, and a scepter shall rise out of Israel; it shall crush the forehead of Moab and break down all the sons of Sheth.* ESV

3:5_____

Rev 3:5   *The one who conquers will be clothed thus in white garments, and I will never blot his name out of the book of life. I will confess his name before my Father and before his angels.* ESV

>   *White garments.
>   *Acknowledge name before God and angels.
>   *Name never removed from the Book of Life.
>   *Book of Life
>   > *First mentioned in Genesis 2 and 3.
>   > *Mentioned in Revelation: 3:5; 13:7-8; 17:8; 20:11-15; 21:27.
>   > *The reference to name being removed may imply that all names are written in the Book of Life at birth. Thus, a name might be removed at some point, e.g. openly rejecting God or dying without being saved.

3:12_____

Rev 3:12   *The one who conquers, I will make him a pillar in the temple of my God. Never shall he go out of it, and I will write on him the name of my God, and the name of the city of my God, the new Jerusalem, which comes down from my God out of heaven, and my own new name.* ESV

>   *Pillar in God's temple.
>   *Never leave temple.
>   *Names written on him.

3:21_____

Rev 3:21   *The one who conquers, I will grant him to sit with me on my throne, as I also conquered and sat down with my Father on his throne.* ESV

>   *Right to sit with God on His throne.

A7. What does it mean that God and the Lamb are the temple in the city?
Revelation 21:22   *And I saw no temple in the city, for its temple is the Lord God the Almighty and the Lamb.* ESV

> *It confirms the Old Testament understanding that the temple was where God resided.

A8. Why does the city not need the sun and the moon?
Revelation 21:23-24   *And the city has no need of sun or moon to shine on it, for the glory of God gives it light, and its lamp is the Lamb. 24 By its light will the nations walk, and the kings of the earth will bring their glory into it.* ESV

> *Because "*the glory of God gives it light, and its lamp is the Lamb.*"
> *In the old Creation, the sun and moon provided the light.
> Q. What does this mean one encounters when they go outside the city?
>
> > *Darkness?
> > *Mystery! This may mean that the light of the New Jerusalem provides light for the surrounding area.

A9. Why is it that only those whose names are written in the Book of Life can be in the city?
Revelation 21:27   *But nothing unclean will ever enter it, nor anyone who does what is detestable or false, but only those who are written in the Lamb's Book of Life.* ESV

> *Because God dwells there and God cannot be in the presence of sin (or sin cannot be in the presence of God).

B. REVELATION 22

B1. What is growing along the side of the river of the water of life?
Revelation 22:2   *through the middle of the street of the city; also, on either side of the river, the tree of life with its twelve kinds of fruit, yielding its fruit each month. The leaves of the tree were for the healing of the nations.* ESV

*The tree of life.

Q. Where do we <u>first</u> encounter the tree of life in Scripture?

> *Gen 2:9   *And out of the ground the Lord God made to spring up every tree that is pleasant to the sight and good for food. The tree of life was in the midst of the garden, and the tree of the knowledge of good and evil. ESV*
>
> *Gen 3:22, 24   Then the Lord God said, "Behold, the man has become like one of us in knowing good and evil. Now, lest he reach out his hand and take also of the tree of life and eat, and live forever . . . 24 He drove out the man, and at the east of the garden of Eden he placed the cherubim and a flaming sword that turned every way to guard the way to the tree of life. ESV*

B2. What does the tree produce?

<u>Revelation 22:2</u>   *through the middle of the street of the city; also, on either side of the river, the tree of life with its twelve kinds of fruit, yielding its fruit each month. The leaves of the tree were for the healing of the nations. ESV*

*Twelve kinds of fruit – monthly.
*Leaves for healing the nations.
Q. Why are healing leaves necessary in this environment?
*<u>Another mystery!</u>
*Ezek 47:12   *And on the banks, on both sides of the river, there will grow all kinds of trees for food. Their leaves will not wither, nor their fruit fail, but they will bear fresh fruit every month, because the water for them flows from the sanctuary. Their fruit will be for food, and their leaves for healing. ESV*
*It is possible that the reference in Rev 22 goes back to Ezekiel 47 (see above). This cannot mean that there will be sickness or death in the New Jerusalem, therefore, it might imply that the river of life produces life because it flows out of the sanctuary.

*It might mean that the divisions that have been between nations have been healed.
*The word "healing" comes from a Greek word where we get the word "therapy." So it could refer to promoting well-being and health.

B3. What is new or different about the first statement in this verse?
<u>Revelation 22:4</u>   *They will see his face* . . . ESV
> *We will see His face. That has never been possible before!
> *This privilege was denied Moses (Ex 33:20, 23).
> *Matt 5:8   *Blessed are the pure in heart, for they shall see God.* ESV

B4. What is the significance of God's name on our foreheads?
<u>Revelation 22:4</u>   . . . *his name will be on their foreheads.* ESV

> *Names revealed the character of the person.
> *We now have the character of God.

B5. Who is the "they" in 22:4 and what do we learn about our responsibilities?
<u>Revelation 22:5</u>   *And night will be no more. They will need no light of lamp or sun, for the Lord God will be their light, and they will reign forever and ever.* ESV

> *"They" means <u>all</u> believers.
> *The Lamb's servants, meaning us.
> *We will reign forever and ever.
> Q. Who are we reigning over?
>> *Not clear. This may not really mean there are other people who have to be reigned over.
>> *It may mean that those with proven leadership skills are leaders in God's eternal Kingdom.

B6. What are we reminded of again?
<u>Revelation 22:8-9</u>   *I, John, am the one who heard and saw these things. And when I heard and saw them, I fell down to worship at the feet of the angel who showed them to me, 9 but he said to me, "You must not do that! I am a fellow servant with you and your*

brothers the prophets, and with those who keep the words of this book. Worship God." ESV

*Do not worship anyone or anything other than God!

B7. Jesus says here that He will give to everyone according to what he or she has done. What does that mean?
Revelation 22:12   Behold, I am coming soon, bringing my recompense with me, to repay everyone for what he has done. ESV
*Judgment.
*2 Cor 5:10   For we must all appear before the judgment seat of Christ, so that each one may receive what is due for what he has done in the body, whether good or evil. ESV
*Matt 16:27   For the Son of Man is going to come with his angels in the glory of his Father, and then he will repay each person according to what he has done. ESV

*Q. Who is the Judge?

*Jesus.
*John 5:22   The Father judges no one, but has given all judgment to the Son. ESV
*2 Cor 5:10: "the judgment seat of Christ."

*Judgment of believers' works
   [probably occurs during the Tribulation on earth]
*1 Cor 3:11-15   For no one can lay a foundation other than that which is laid, which is Jesus Christ. 12 Now if anyone builds on the foundation with gold, silver, precious stones, wood, hay, straw— 13 each one's work will become manifest, for the Day will disclose it, because it will be revealed by fire, and the fire will test what sort of work each one has done. 14 If the work that anyone has built on the foundation survives, he will receive a reward. 15 If anyone's work is burned up, he will suffer loss, though he himself will be saved, but only as through fire. ESV

*Purpose
*Judgment for rewards (not sins).
*Based on works.

*Specific rewards mentioned in Scripture
*Bringing people to Christ (1 Thes 2:19). [difficult to interpret]
*Loving Christ's appearing (2 Tim 4:8).

*Endure testing with love for Jesus (James 1:12).
*Elders who are faithful to the church (1 Pet 5:1-4).

*Conclusion:
*What we do with our lives here on earth may determine for all eternity our privileges, status, and responsibility in Heaven.

B8. What are we told again here?
Revelation 22:14-15   *Blessed are those who wash their robes, so that they may have the right to the tree of life and that they may enter the city by the gates. 15 Outside are the dogs and sorcerers and the sexually immoral and murderers and idolaters, and everyone who loves and practices falsehood.* ESV

*Only those who wash their robes in the blood of the Lamb will be allowed into the city and have access to the tree of life. All others are separated from God, outside the city gates, where there may not be light.
*Rev 7:14   *I said to him, "Sir, you know." And he said to me, "These are the ones coming out of the great tribulation. They have washed their robes and made them white in the blood of the Lamb."* ESV

*Remember: Rev 7:14 refers to the great multitude in the throne room who are wearing white robes.

B9. What is Jesus' last promise and what does it mean?
Revelation 22:20   *He who testifies to these things says, "Surely I am coming soon." Amen. Come, Lord Jesus!* ESV

*I am coming soon.
*Jesus says this three times in Chapter 22.
*The implication is His coming is imminent.
*It may mean when He comes it will be quickly.

B10. What appeals most to you about living in the New Jerusalem, other than being in the presence of God?

*No more sin!

C. APPLICATION

C1. So where do you want to be: in the lake of fire or the new Jerusalem?

>   *A very easy choice.

C2. Are you an overcomer?

C3. Is your name in the Book of Life? How do you know?

C4. What is the absolute minimum that needs to be done in order to be saved and arrive at the new Jerusalem?

>   *Believe (have faith) that Jesus is the Son of God.
>   *Confess and repent of your sins.
>   *Accept or receive Him as Savior and Lord.

Transformation Road Map
Primary Takeaways

THE BEGINNING

1: Despite human failings, God's redemptive plan is available to all believers, offering hope and restoration through faith in His promises.

2: Obedience to God's commands and a forward-focused faith are essential. Looking back or clinging to worldly attachments can lead to spiritual ruin.

3: Unwavering loyalty to God and steadfast resistance to temptation, even in the face of adversity, are essential for fulfilling God's greater plan in one's life.

4: In the story of The Flood we find that unwavering obedience to God's commands, even in the face of widespread disbelief and ridicule, leads to salvation and blessings.

THE END

5: Unrelenting faith and obedience to God's calling, even with extreme opposition and persecution, can have a powerful impact and ultimately lead to divine vindication and victory.

6: Remain vigilant against the allure of worldly power, wealth, and false teachings. Hold steadfast in one's devotion to God, resisting the temptations of spiritual adultery and apostasy.

7: Worship and recognition of God's creation and sustenance of all things should be a constant principle of a believer's heart and life. He is worthy!

8: Remaining separate from the world's corrupting influences, which prioritize material wealth and self-indulgence over God, is crucial for maintaining spiritual purity and avoiding judgment.

Free PDF
MAKE WISE DECISIONS
[Get the ebook version for 99 cents]

Consequences Shape Lives.

This book discusses the nature of decisions and explores eight essential questions to make better decisions.

You are a few decisions away from transforming your life. You can make better decisions! This resource has sections on what makes a poor decision, questions to ask yourself, traps to avoid, short and sweet decisions, the wise decision framework, and twenty ways to be wise. It also has a handy decision-making checklist. (12 pages)

Free PDF: https://getwisdompublishing.com/resource-registration/

Kindle ebook for 99 cents: https://www.amazon.com/dp/B0FG8NC53J

Ebook

MAKE WISE DECISIONS

Consequences Shape Lives

Stephen H Berkey
J. S. Wellman

Free PDF

Ten Steps to Wise Choices

Timeless Wisdom. Practical Tools. Lasting Impact.

Free PDF
Life Improvement Principles
[Get the ebook version for 99 cents]

You can live your best life!

Welcome to a journey of discovery! In case you have forgotten, your actions have consequences. Unlock your potential! This book (60+ pages) provides the overview of all our strategies and wisdom principles to live your best life. You *can* transform your life! Get your wisdom-based roadmap to a better life and unlock all the possibilities for growth and success.

Free PDF: https://getwisdompublishing.com/resource-registration/

Kindle ebook for 99 cents:
https://www.amazon.com/dp/B0FG883KZM

Ebook

Free PDF

Make it your life goal to be the best you can be!

Discover Wisdom and live the life you deserve.

Next Steps!

Continue Studying the *OBSCURE* Series
The *OBSCURE* Bible Study Series
https://www.amazon.com/dp/B08T7TL1B1

Be Challenged by the Jesus Follower Series
The Jesus Follower Bible Study Series
https://www.amazon.com/dp/B0DHP39P5J

Tackle Wisdom-Driven Life Change
Apply Biblical Wisdom to Live Your Best Life!
"Effective Life Change"
https://www.amazon.com/dp/1952359732

Know What You Should Pray
Personal Daily Prayer Guide
https://www.amazon.com/What-Should-Pray-Personal-Journal/dp/1952359260/

Decide to be the Very Best You Can Be
The Life Planning Series
https://www.amazon.com/dp/B09TH9SYC4

You Can Help:
SOCIAL MEDIA: Mention The *OBSCURE* Bible Study Series on your social platforms. Include the hashtag #obscurebiblestudy so we are aware of your post.

FRIENDS: Recommend *OBSCURE* to your family, friends, small group, Sunday School class leaders, or your church.

REVIEW: Please give us your honest review at
https://www.amazon.com/dp/1734409495

The *OBSCURE* Bible Study Series

Continue your journey through the hidden
wisdom of Scripture with the OBSCURE Series.

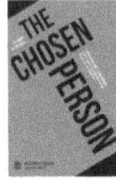

Blasphemy, Grace, Quarrels & Reconciliation: The lives of first-century disciples.
This book presents Joseph of Arimathea, Joanna, Ananias, Hymenaeus, and Cornelius (a centurion). It illustrates the nature and challenges of life as a first-century disciple.

The Beginning and the End: From creation to eternity.
This book has four lessons from Genesis and four from Revelation covering creation, rebellion, grace, worship, and eternity. God is leading us to worship in the Throne Room.

God at the Center: He is sovereign and I am not.
This book examines the virgin birth, worship, prayer, the sovereignty of God, compromise, and trust. God is at the center of all these stories. He is at the center of our lives.

Women of Courage: God did some serious business with these women.
This book examines the lives of Jael, Rizpah, the woman of Tekoa, Tabitha, Shiphrah, and Lydia. These women exhibit great courage and faithfulness. God used them in amazing ways.

The Beginning of Wisdom: Your personal character counts.
In this book we find courage, loyalty, thankfulness, love, forgiveness, and humility. Personal character counts. Decisions have consequences. Wisdom will help us stand firm in our faith.

Miracles & Rebellion: The good, the bad, and the indifferent.
God hates sin and loves to heal the faithful. The rebellion of Korah, Haman, and Alexander compare to the healing stories of Aeneas, a slave girl, and the crippled man at Lystra.

The Chosen People: There is a remnant.
This book concentrates mostly on Israel in the Old Testament, but also covers some interesting subjects as Lucifer, Michael the archangel, and Job's wife.

The Chosen Person: Keep your eyes on Jesus.
The focus is on Jesus and the superiority of Christ. We investigate Melchizedek, the disciples on the road to Emmaus, Nicodemus, and the criminal on the cross.

WEBSITE: http://getwisdompublishing.com/products/
AMAZON: www.amazon.com/author/stephenhberkey

Jesus Follower Bible Study Series

The Jesus Follower Bible Study Series will provide you with a complete description of the nature, characteristics, obligations, commitments, and responsibilities of a true Jesus follower.

Go to our Amazon Book Series page for your copy:

https://www.amazon.com/dp/B0DHP39P5J

The RELATIONSHIP CHARACTERISTICS of a Jesus Follower:
　　　Are you right with God?
The ONE ANOTHER INSTRUCTIONS to a Jesus Follower:
　　　Are you right with one another?
The WORSHIP of a Jesus Follower:
　　　Is your worship acceptable or in vain?
The PRAYER of a Jesus Follower:
　　　What Scripture says about unleashing the power of God.
The DANGERS of SIN for a Jesus Follower:
　　　God HATES sin! He abhors sin!
The FOCUS for a Jesus Follower:
　　　Keep your eyes fixed on Jesus!
The HEART Requirements of a Jesus Follower:
　　　Follow with all your heart, mind, body, and soul!
The COMMITMENTS of a Jesus Follower:
　　　Practical Christian living and discipleship.
The OBEDIENCE Requirements for a Jesus Follower:
　　　Ignore at your own risk!

"Get Wisdom Publishing creates wisdom-driven products that equip readers with timeless insights, understanding, and actionable tools to transform their lives."

Life Planning Series

Read these books if you want to live a better life.
The primary audience for this series is the secular self-help market, but the concepts are Christian based.

CHOOSE FAITH	**For the spiritual seeker and those with spiritual questions.** *Your Spiritual Guidebook For Questions About Religion, God, Heaven, Truth, Evil, and the Afterlife.* https://www.amazon.com/dp/1952359473
CHOOSE CORE VALUES	**Core values will drive your life.** https://www.amazon.com/dp/195235949X

Other Titles in the Life Planning Series
CHOOSE Integrity
CHOOSE Friends Wisely
CHOOSE The Right Words
CHOOSE Good Work Habits
CHOOSE Financial Responsibility
CHOOSE A Positive Self-Image
CHOOSE Leadership
CHOOSE Love and Family
LIFE PLANNING HANDBOOK A Life Plan Is The Key To Personal Growth https://www.amazon.com/gp/product/1952359325

Go to:
https://www.amazon.com/dp/B09TH9SYC4
to get these books.

Personal Daily Prayer Guide
Prayer Resource and Journal

This is a great resource to kick-start your prayer life!

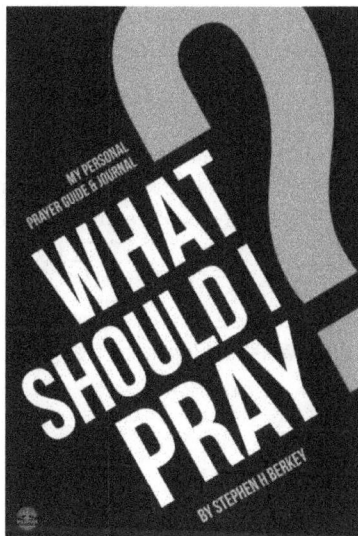

Know what to pray.
Pray based on Bible verses.
Strengthen your prayer life.
Access reference resources.
Pray with eternal implications.
Write your own prayers if desired.
Organize and focus your prayer time.
Learn what the Bible says about prayer.
Find encouragement and advice on how to pray.
Reduce frustration and distraction in your prayer time.

Get your copy today!

https://www.amazon.com/What-Should-Pray-Personal-Journal/dp/1952359260/

Acknowledgments

Arlene
Arlene has served as wife, editor, and proof-reader for all of my writing – thank you for your patience, help, and love.

Michelle
Michelle, our older daughter, has been an invaluable resource. She has graciously produced the website at www.getwisdompublishing.com. She was the first author in the family: graceandthegravelroad.com.

Stephanie
Our middle daughter designed all the covers for the *OBSCURE* Bible Study Series, as well as the marks and logos for Get Wisdom Publishing. We are grateful for her talent!

KOINONIA Small Group
These dear friends have hung in there with me as I taught many of the lessons to them first. Their input, answers, and suggestions have been invaluable.

God, Jesus, and Holy Spirit
Thank you, Lord, for Your guidance and direction.

Notes

1. Nelson's Illustrated Bible Dictionary, Copyright © 1986, Thomas Nelson Publishers; from PC Study Bible, "Walk"

2. Nelson's Illustrated Bible Dictionary, Copyright © 1986, Thomas Nelson Publishers; from PC Study Bible, "Antichrist"

About the Author

Steve attended church as a child and accepted Christ when he was 10 years old. But his walk with Jesus left a lot to be desired for the next 44 years. In 1994 he "wrestled" with God for some period of months and in September of that year totally surrendered his life to Jesus.

In 1996 he was so driven to study God's Word that he attended the Indianapolis campus of Trinity Evangelical Divinity School (Chicago) to earn a Certificate of Biblical Studies. His hunger for God's Word led him to lead and write all his own Bible studies for his small group. He has been an entrepreneur and Bible study leader for the past 30 years.

He is a member of The Church at Station Hill in Spring Hill, TN, a regional campus of Brentwood Baptist (Brentwood TN).

GET**WISDOM**
P U B L I S H I N G

www.getwisdompublishing.com

"Get Wisdom Publishing is dedicated to being the trusted source of wisdom-driven books that inspire growth, guide decisions, and empower readers to live with purpose and fulfillment."

Contact Us

Website: www.getwisdompublishing.com

Email: info@getwisdompublishing.com

Facebook: Get Wisdom Publishing

Author's Page: www.amazon.com/author/stephenhberkey

Amazon's Obscure Bible Study Series page:
https://www.amazon.com/dp/B08T7TL1B1

"Go beyond devotionals.
Experience biblical wisdom in action!"